I WISH SOMEONE UNDERSTOOD MY DIVORCE

A Practical Cope-Book

Harold Ivan Smith

AUGSBURG Publishing House • Minneapolis

I WISH SOMEONE UNDERSTOOD MY DIVORCE
A Practical Cope-Book

Copyright © 1986 Augsburg Publishing House

Scripture quotations unless otherwise noted are from the Holy Bible: New International Version. Copyright 1978 by the New York International Bible Society. Used by permission of Zondervan Bible Publishers.

First names only are used with most of the stories told in this book. Unless otherwise noted, these names are fictitious and the specific details of the stories have been altered so as to make the characters unrecognizable.

Library of Congress Cataloging-in-Publication Data

Smith, Harold Ivan.
   I WISH SOMEONE UNDERSTOOD MY DIVORCE.

   Bibliography: p.
   1. Divorced people—United States—Psychology.
2. Separation (Psychology)   I. Title.
HQ834.T684   1986   306.8'9   86-28874
ISBN 0-8066-2246-6

Manufactured in the U.S.A.   APH 10-3194

        3   4   5   6   7   8   9   0   1   2   3   4   5   6   7   8   9

CONTENTS

Preface   **7**

Part One: It's Happening!   **11**

1   "I Can't Believe It!"   11
2   Experience the Pain   15
3   One Day at a Time   18
4   Tomorrow Begins Today   20
5   "I Can Make It"   22

Part Two: "I Wish Someone Understood"   **24**

6   "I Wish I Understood"   24
7   "I Wish My Mate Understood"   26
8   "I Wish My Children Understood"   28
9   "I Wish My Parents Understood"   30
10   "I Wish Our Friends Understood"   32
11   "I Wish Our Neighbors Understood"   35
12   "I Wish My Employer Understood"   38
13   "I Wish My Pastor Understood"   41

Part Three: Barriers to Understanding   **44**

14   The Editing Barrier   44
15   The Silence Barrier   46
16   The Uniqueness Barrier   48
17   The Martyrdom Barrier   49
18   The Shame Barrier   51
19   The Pride Barrier   53

Part Four: Dealing with Fears   **56**

20   The Fear Landscape   56
21   Fear of Myself   59
22   Fear of Change   61
23   Fear of Losing My Children   63
24   Fear of Losing My Friends   67
25   Fear of Rejection   69
26   Fear of Damnation   71
27   Fear of Not Surviving   74
28   Fear of Being Poor   75
29   Fear of Being Alone   79
30   Fear of Holidays   81

Part Five: Priorities for Living   **84**

31   Recognizing Your Vulnerability   84
32   Reestablishing Your Identity   87
33   Reexamining Your Priorities   89
34   Restating Your Values   93
35   Relinquishing False Innocence   95
36   Reducing Your Manipulability   99
37   Rejecting the "You-Talk"   102
38   Recognizing Dead-Ends   104
39   Refurbishing Your Self-Image   107
40   Realigning Guilt and Responsibility   110
41   Resisting the "Demons"   112
42   Resisting Bargain-Basement Life-Styles   114
43   Resuming Custody   116
44   Repairing the Damage   119
45   Recovering from Bad Decisions   121
46   Redeeming the Experience   123
47   Renewing Your Faith   125
48   Reaffirming Your Value   127

49 Reclaiming Your Dream   129
50 Reserving the Best   131
51 Reducing the Emotional Baggage   133
52 Renegotiating Your Future   135

Part Six: Resources for Renewal   **138**

53 Baby Steps   138
54 Counseling   139
55 A Friend   142
56 Time   144
57 A Support Group   146
58 A Vacation   148
59 Exercise   151
60 Reading   154

Afterword: Your Divorce Can Make a Difference   **156**

Notes   **158**

PREFACE

"I wish someone understood what I'm going through!"

I've heard that sentence a thousand times. In soft, southern drawl, in crisp New England speech, in broken English by immigrants and Hispanic aliens.

I've sensed it in people who were crying too hard to talk or who fumbled with their hands when their lips and brains would not cooperate.

I've said it myself, many times. I've slapped the steering wheel of my car. I've pounded a doorjamb or two. I've soaked my pillow, mumbling the sentence.

Some say it with a sense of disbelief. Old men, young women. Grandfathers. Young men—too young to have been married and divorced already, fighting with every ounce of machismo to cut off the tears.

I've hugged them. Squeezed them. Whispered, "It's going to be all right," or "Everything's going to work out, you'll see."

It's not that there aren't people who can understand. Some try— really try. My counselor was one of the honest ones. Hugh said, "Harold, there's no way I can really understand what you are going through. So I won't try. But I am going to try to listen to you. And maybe between the two of us. . . ."

A friend, Dr. Gordon Wetmore, tells about the time as a young minister he went to see a parishioner who was dying. In her hospital room he approached the woman, who was wracked with hideous pain. He took her hand and called her by name and then mumbled a phrase he had learned in seminary: "I understand what you are going through. . . ."

Instantly, her eyes snapped open.

"Young man," she gasped, "you have no earthly idea what I am going through!"

He squirmed, but she tightened her grasp on his hand.

"No," he finally admitted, embarrassed by the inadequacy of the cliché. But he stayed for an hour and listened to her. That experience changed him.

That's *our* problem, too. We've been patted on the head, like a child with a stubbed toe. "Now, now—it can't be all that bad." Yes, it can!

Or have you encountered those who say, "If you had taken my advice, you wouldn't be in this mess. . .."?

Or have you been assaulted by a Bible-totin', Bible-quotin', perhaps well-meaning person who thundered, "Divorced? Well, God hates divorce!" or "The Bible says. . .."? It's always the tone of voice that nails you.

Or there's the one who had the quiet, amicable divorce and can't understand what you're so emotional about. Or the one whose smoldering anger erupts. Whose anger frightens you. You think, *I hope I don't end up like that!*

How many times did I try to explain, only to become frustrated and give up? How many times did I scold myself: "I'm not making any sense, am I?"

There were times I thought I would die. Times when I would have given everything in my bank account to someone who understood. Times when I ruined parties, or dinners, with words— with my grief. Times when I caught the glances people exchanged—when I made them uncomfortable. Times when I saw them glance at their watches and wonder if I was about through. Times when I sensed their longing to escape.

And I remember the times I prayed, "O God, if only someone understood. . . ."

I've been so desperate that I have:

- apologetically called friends at 2:00 A.M.;
- poured out my grief to total strangers;
- paced motel rooms like a zoo-bound tiger;
- locked my hands around my legs and rocked back and forth;
- plotted my own death.

There are 220 million people in this country—and I thought none of them understood.

Then I met one who did, and then another. And slowly I learned to translate, to communicate. And after sobbing and blowing my nose, I've sat in stunned silence, in awe, relieved because someone finally understood. There were times when I rushed to embrace them, trying to find an adequate way to say, "Thank you."

From a Nazi prison cell, Dietrich Bonhoeffer wrote, "The first duty we owe a man is to listen to him." I agree.

I'm going to share with you some of my own experience: the detours, the U-turns, the backtracking, the snarls.

I'm going to share some things I have learned from the thousands of courageous people who have attended my single-adult seminars.

Not every page may apply to you (although some might help you understand someone else). Skip around. Read what speaks to *you, now,* in your own situation.

There may be times when I will bump up against something sensitive. It's OK to put the book down for awhile. I understand.

But remember, you'd be angry at a dentist who wasn't thorough, one who said, "Well, you were squirming, so I thought I wouldn't finish. . . ." I'll do my best to be gentle.

If it hurts too much, put the book down—go for a walk, do

some sit-ups, get a fresh cup of coffee, munch a cookie, water a plant. The book will still be here when you come back.

Here is a growth principle:

You have dignity . . . worth . . . value. You are special. And you have a tomorrow ahead that has your initials monogrammed on it.

I have included growth principles with most of the sections of this book. Some you will want to memorize. From time to time, flip back through the book, rereading the growth principles. They will refresh your memory and your commitment to a tomorrow that is better than today.

Once upon a time, I had all the answers on the question of divorce. As a graduate student in religion, I had it all figured out. Matthew 19 presented no problems for me. Divorce was wrong—to be avoided at all costs.

Then I became one of "those people."

I'm not an expert.

I haven't finished my journey.

It still hurts on a rainy Sunday afternoon.

I'm still discovering new growth principles.

But if you're ready, I'm ready. Turn the page. Let's get started.

Part One

IT'S HAPPENING!

1 "I Can't Believe It!"

"What happened?"

That may be a question you ask yourself frequently these days. Everyone expects you to be able to explain. A few want you to justify your actions.

It is important that you find a way to tell your story, to assemble as many of the facts, impressions, and even "unexplainables" as possible. It's important to try to make sense out of pieces that do not necessarily make sense.

Sometimes two and two do not add up to four.

You may have had a grinding-down experience, or perhaps a chain reaction. "I did this, then he did this . . . then. . . ." Some of us were overwhelmed by what Eugene Kennedy calls "the black-and-blue traumas of ordinary living."[1]

There seems to be a pattern—not for everyone, but for many. First there is dazed confusion. The divorcing person cannot fully explain all the factors involved to his or her satisfaction or to the satisfaction of those sitting on the sidelines. This reality leads to more misunderstanding and confusion and feeds the rumor mills. As a result, many divorced people fall into a "Nobody knows the trouble I've seen. . ." syndrome.

When we have a problem in sharing our experience with others, it is generally a language problem and not a problem with the thoughts behind the language. Deep down, we know what we mean. Yet we fumble for words.

Look at this common progression:

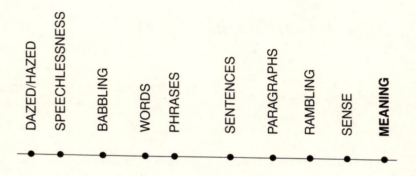

There is the initial *dazed moment.* "This can't be happening! At least not to me!" As if to convince ourselves, we rattle off several reasons:

- We're Christians.
- We just bought a house.
- We have three children.
- We're happy.
- Divorce only happens to *other* people.

Some, however, can only mumble, "Oh, my God!" A few do not even have the strength to add the exclamation mark. Many quickly begin to deny that what is happening is really happening. Or they may accept that it is happening but deny any lasting impact: "He/she will have to change his/her mind" or "come around." And there are some who don't get too upset about a separation.

Others are *speechless*. It's like walking out on stage and realizing you have no lines. They are stunned. There is a benefit from this reaction, however. You avoid saying anything that complicates the problem, like "Good riddance!" or "Don't come back!"

Unfortunately, some mates misinterpret such speechlessness as a lack of caring.

"What did he say when you left?"

"Nothing. He just looked at me."

Some reconciliations have been made much more difficult by harsh, angry words, perhaps long suppressed, but which exploded like gunfire at a departing spouse.

Babbling is the next stage. The motive is not so much to foster communication as it is to gain emotional relief. "It's like an elephant sitting on my chest," one man explained. "I thought I was going to suffocate."

Listen to the babbling (we call it jabbering) of a child. The purpose is to rehearse the sounds—to learn to construct words and sentences that will communicate.

Babbling is unrestrained verbiage. Words and ideas just pour out, or even hemorrhage. The words may even be subconscious rather than deliberate. Sometimes the speaker fears rejection by the listener. He or she may try to get out as much as possible before that happens.

The encouragement of a sympathetic and patient listener at this point can make an incredible difference. The moment a divorced person realizes someone is really listening, there may be a sense of liberation.

We start with hurt and pain. That evolves into simple phrases: "I hurt . . . I feel bad. . . ." Slowly the speaker adds adjectives.

Eventually the phrases become sentences, and then paragraphs. But here a new problem arises. Just as listeners are thwarted by mumbling, they may now struggle with too much data—motor-mouthing.

"Whoa! Slow down!" the listener pleads. "Did I hear you say . . .?" is the question of a wise listener. But some are waiting for you to get to the "good parts," especially if sex is involved.

Once they start using sentences and paragraphs, some separated or divorced people ramble—jumping across logical time sequences and changes in speaker. In a novel an author has to put in a few "he said/she saids" to make things clear. Sometimes listeners have to interrupt and say, "Wait—who said what?"

Some people will have difficulty following the sequence of events. For one thing, there may be a big difference between our version and our mate's version of events and conversations.

Finally, some sense emerges. Out of the pain, shame, hurt, wounding, frustration, and chaos, a person begins to make sense. We almost feel a sense of pride.

But we're also afraid of being misunderstood. We don't want people thinking we're basket cases. That intensifies our struggles with words. Are we also afraid to show our vulnerabilities, blunders, and sins?

In my seminars, people sometimes fumble with words and then stop. When I sense that frustration I urge them to continue.

"I don't know how to say it. . . ."

"Then just say it the way you're thinking it. I'll help you sort it out."

This *is* happening to you. Somehow you have to make sense of it, for the benefit of both you and your family.

It's important to know:

- *What* do I tell?
- *When* do I tell it?

- *Whom* do I tell it to?
- *Why* do I tell it?
- *Where* do I tell it?

You may know what you are thinking and be able to express yourself. But the struggle may be in finding words and phrases that will translate into the experience of your listener.

How do we help someone to understand us, or at least to take a step toward understanding us? That's what this book is all about.

2   Experience the Pain

"I feel like a firehouse," remarked one divorced man, "in which all the firebells are ringing and I don't know which one to answer first."

Others have expressed the initial moments as insanity. "I thought I was going crazy!"

Another wrote, "I wanted to die. It would have been so much easier to have *buried* my wife."

Psychologist Frank Freed often asks his clients, "What are you pretending not to know?" That's a good question for us to ask as well.

Jim Smoke maintains that there are some alternatives to fully experiencing a divorce:

- Did you *avoid* your divorce (mentally or emotionally)?
- Did you *escape* your divorce (a quick new marriage)?
- Did you *deny* your divorce ("It didn't happen.")?

But the big question is still, "Are you willing to *face* your divorce?" and keep facing it?[2]

Opera doesn't overwhelm me. A few times I have wanted to leave after Act I. But my opera-loving friend patted my arm and whispered, "It ain't over until the fat lady sings!" So I stayed. If I had left at the intermission, I would have missed something. Act II made sense of Act I; Act III made sense of Acts I and II. If you try to skip part of the experience that goes with your divorce, you will miss an opportunity to make sense of the whole.

It's important to experience the pain, to stare this thing in the face. It will be easy to cop out. There will be plenty of cut-rate alternatives: alcohol, work, sex. There will be those who will home in on your "wounded" radar signals: "Honey, I know just what you need!" You may be surprised at who says that to you.

You will soon face a fork in the road. An important decision you must make is what kind of language you will use during and after your divorce. You will catch yourself using "we" after years of marital habit. It's difficult to get used to saying "I."

You will also have to choose between a decision-based life-style and an authority-based life-style. A decision-based life-style is potential-based, while an authority-based life-style is feeling-based. A decision life-style has one key phrase; an authority-based life-style has several.

DECISION-BASED LIFE-STYLE	AUTHORITY-BASED LIFE-STYLE
• I can	• I must • I should • I ought • I had better

People who have decision-based life-styles recognize they have permission to do something. People who have authority-based life-styles look for someone or something to give them permission.

"I can" brings freedom, and with freedom comes responsibilities. Authority-based life-stylers look for people to make their decisions for them, but they are the ones who still have to live with the consequences.

Consider the sexual arena. All of us have sexual needs. Decision-based life-stylers will admit them and accept them; authority-based life-stylers may deny or camouflage their needs.

Decision-based life-stylers face their hormones and may choose to be celibate. Authority-based life-stylers say, "I *have* to be celibate or. . .

- I might get herpes.
- I might get pregnant/get someone pregnant.
- I might get AIDS.
- I might . . . bring about miscellaneous dire consequences.

Decision-based life-stylers know they have permission to make choices and to accept the consequences of those choices.

Authority-based life-stylers look for people to grant them permission or to make their decisions for them (and people to blame if the decision doesn't work out).

Many of us go through life not as POWs but as POSs: prisoners-of-shoulds!

There is danger in freedom and in "I can." It may lead to license and recklessness. But an authority-based life-style can lead to neuroses and repression. Denis Waitley noted, "The only limitations you will ever face will be those you place on yourself."[3] The Creator gave us incredible power

. . . when he gave us the ability to choose. Power means having the ability to choose among the many possibilities open to us and the freedom to act upon them in order to shape the direction of our lives.[4]

Millions of people have faced defeat and yet have still mumbled or muttered or screamed, "I can. . . ."

There is a fork in the road. One sign points to "I can." The other points to "I should." It's your choice. You *can* decide your future in that intersection.

In school I often had to do "write-offs" for misbehavior: "I will not talk! I will not talk! I will not talk!" 250 boring times.

I have a simple assignment for you. It's a write-off. Fill in the spaces below with the first thing that comes to your mind. It may be outrageous. It may be stupid. Fine. Write it down.

- I can _____ .
- I can _____ .
- I can _____ .
- I can _____ .
- I can _____ .

You can eliminate "I must" and "I should" and "I ought to" from your vocabulary. Today is a good day to start.

You can survive and thrive—even through a divorce. Today is a good day to start.

3   One Day at a Time

"I waited patiently for the Lord; he turned to me and heard my cry" (Ps. 40:1).

The Saturday westerns I used to watch on TV occasionally had a hanging or near-hanging scene. Sometimes an angry mob would get very close to lynching an innocent man—and sometimes they succeeded. Yet some men were saved at the last minute—even after the noose had been tightened around their necks.

Maybe that's how you feel today. You can feel the noose tightening. Time seems to be running out, and no help is in sight.

You can cope at the end of your rope!

It's easy for divorced people to say, "But what can I *do*?" Some have learned helpless behavior as a way of gaining sympathy or avoiding responsibility.

Do you remember Tom Sawyer's resourcefulness? He wanted to go fishing, but first he had to whitewash the fence. Tom coped with his predicament by coming up with a great idea. He got several friends to help him with his work.

Copers rarely hit the panic button. They say or shout, "Let me think a minute! There's got to be a way out of this." After a while you notice the smile or hear the finger snap. "Got it!"

Panic can be deadly. It's almost impossible to create good solutions when you are panicked.

Some people have coped so well that we don't know that they have ever been married and divorced. At some point they have chosen to "befriend" their divorces. They have chosen not to exhaust themselves fighting against the current. They have followed sound advice: Relax. "Wait for the Lord" (Ps. 27:14).

Mary is a 34-year-old who has learned to cope with her divorce. Initially she went through a major depression. Now she works a full day. By carefully following doctor's orders and staying sensitive to her body's warning signals, she is no longer dependent on drugs. She has learned to live alone and to continue to work hard, yet she still makes time to participate in social and church activities.

Mary started with small choices during her divorce and depression. She likes to give money to organizations that help feed hungry people. Before she learned to cope, she often stayed in bed the entire day. She refused to stare down her depression. She played and replayed the "poor me" tapes. Many days she didn't go to work. (Only a tolerant employer saved her job.)

Then Mary received a note from a social service agency explaining how her small contributions helped them feed hungry and homeless people. She realized that if she stayed in bed, she couldn't work. And if she didn't work, she wouldn't have money to contribute to others. Somewhere a hungry child needed her.

At those moments when Mary is tempted to pull the covers over her head, she now looks at a small, framed photo on the nightstand. That picture of a starving child reminds her that he, too, has needs.

Coping is a choice that is available to you—even if you are divorced. Even if your divorce is the worst in history, remember: you cope *one day at a time!*

4   *Tomorrow Begins Today*

After one of my seminars a woman came up to me offering her compliments.

"Oh, you helped me so much."

"Thank you."

"You know so much about divorce."

"Thank you." Tears welled up in her eyes. A recent divorcée, I quickly concluded. "How long has it been?" I asked.

"Seventeen years," she said softly.

"Seventeen years? Did you say, 'seventeen years'? Listen, if you can't get over it in seventeen years, you won't get any help from me!"

Others in my seminars ask, "How long does it take to get over a divorce?" My answer is simple: *as long as you take!*

Making room for tomorrow frequently means changing your perspective. The real question is, when does that opportunity come? Denis Waitley says tomorrow begins:

- when you stop tearing yourself down;
- when you stop worrying about what other people think or are saying;
- when you stop imagining how everything could go wrong;
- when you stop fretting about past failures.[5]

To these I would add:

- when you start running toward tomorrow as fast as you did from your past;
- when you start seeing today as a step toward tomorrow;
- when you start accepting yourself as you are, right now, warts and all;
- when you start realizing that happiness begins now;
- when you realize the present is not permanent.

Everyone—whether single, married, or divorced—is given the same amount of time in a day to get tomorrow launched:

- 24 hours, or
- 1,440 minutes, or
- 86,400 seconds.

You can always moan and groan about how hard it is to make a decision or to get started, but the clock is ticking just the same. When your 86,400 seconds are gone, they're gone. And then tomorrow is here and you will still face the same hurdles.

"Where do I go to find my tomorrow?" is what many ask themselves. The myth implicit in this statement is that tomorrow is somewhere else—some distant point around the bend, some place described in a full-color poster or travel brochure, somewhere—anywhere—other than your present address and zip code.

Tomorrow always starts where you are today.

One decision ignites tomorrow. Regardless of how battered, confused, or angry you may be, *you* are the one who decides when your tomorrow begins!

You don't have to ask anyone's permission.

If your goal is growth (and I hope it is), ask yourself, "How can I spend my time *today* achieving that which will launch my *tomorrow*?" You'll find some suggestions on how to do that in Part Five of this book.

Tomorrow begins today.

5   *"I Can Make It!"*

You can make it! It is possible for you to be a victor over your divorce instead of a victim.

You may say, "It might have worked for him, but it won't work for *me!*" You may even tick off three or four reasons why not.

I can understand why you are somewhat reluctant to believe me. But what are your alternatives?

- to get even?
- to whine?
- to be a martyr?

Wouldn't it be better to be a winner?

Genesis 1:2 says, "The earth was formless and empty, darkness was over the surface of the deep. . . ." As I write this, I am enjoying the beauty of the mountains of the eastern part of Washington state. I watched the autumn sun set over the sparkling waters of the Spokane River. Yet all this was once void—without form or beauty.

Yet out of the chaos, God created beauty.

What about your chaos? your void? your darkness?

While there is nothing that you can do about yesterday, you can anticipate tomorrow. Don't waste today. It's precious.

Be patient. There are no instant recoveries. You need time to heal. Some injuries bring on complications because an impatient patient doesn't allow enough time for healing. Give yourself permission to take as much time as you need.

And remember: yours is not the first or probably the last divorce. Sure, you will stub a few toes and make some bloopers. But someone, somewhere has it worse than you do. You'll discover how true this is when you join a divorce recovery group. There you'll find people who can help you—your cheerleaders and encouragers. They may be bank tellers, construction workers, cashiers, dental hygienists, or teachers. But they will be individuals who have faced "the impossible," who have found the *possible* in "the impossible." They will insist, "If I can make it, *you* can make it!"

There will be times when it will sound insane to say, "I can make it." Most evidence may point to the opposite conclusion:

- You're two months behind in your rent.
- Your ex thinks alimony is voluntary.
- Your kids are rebelling.
- Your car is sputtering.

But others have made it, and so can you!

It's always too early to give up!

Part Two

"I WISH SOMEONE UNDERSTOOD"

---
6   *"I Wish I Understood"*

Just when you think you have it all figured out, something comes along to confuse you.

Many people assume that a divorce is like a 500-piece, interlocking jigsaw puzzle. If I can just get the borders done, then I am halfway there. So we group pieces together. But then you sit there, holding a piece of the puzzle that seemingly fits nowhere! Some people become impatient with jigsaw puzzles. So they "force" pieces to fit—with a smack of the palm.

I've fussed and fumed with a puzzle, only to have someone come up, take the piece from my hand, and snap it into place. And I have sat there dumbfounded.

Divorce is not always logical. Often there are no borders to the puzzle, and worse, no picture on the cover of the box to use as a guide. Yet slowly, piece by piece, the puzzle begins to take shape.

We may chuckle at how easy it is as we fit piece after piece into its place. Then we get stuck.

I remember thinking I had to be a Columbo—to figure out what was happening or had happened. I reasoned that only then could I plot an effective strategy for reconciliation. Too many divorced people get cerebral or analytical. Unfortunately, as a result they ignore one key reality—a divorce doesn't always make sense (at least, not at the time).

You won't be able to figure it all out by yourself. You will need the help of others: counselors, friends, a support group. Sometimes these "helpers" provide a missing piece of the puzzle.

Sometimes I've suddenly interrupted people and said, "Say that again!" Many times they were surprised—and then flustered as they tried to remember what they had said.

Here are some common barriers to understanding:

- Someone may be deliberately depriving you of information essential for understanding.
- You may be too busy denying the experience to accept reality.
- You may be pretending not to know crucial facts.
- You may be too frightened by long-term consequences.
- You may be anesthetized (drugs/liquor/sex/a new relationship).
- You may be too busy (solutions require big chunks of silence).
- You may need a change of scenery, a time-out.
- You may be too busy blaming, playing the role of victim.

Sometimes we have to turn out the light, fluff the pillow, and say, "Tomorrow will bring me another step closer to understanding this." A good night's sleep can do wonders to make us more open to understanding.

7   *"I Wish My Mate Understood"*

For a long time, I thought "someone" would come along and take Jane's place in my life and heart. I would simply cross out Jane and insert a new name. It hasn't happened yet.

Eighty-five percent of divorced men marry within 14 months of the gavel (some much sooner). Women generally wait longer.

As a result, some have not had time to conclude the grief process. They expect the excitement, particularly sexual, of a new relationship to keep their grief at arm's length.

Others know all is not well and frantically work to hide it— like a child trying to keep a beach ball under water. It can be done, but if you aren't careful the ball will come swooshing up out of the water. And if you have denied that you had it in the first place, people can become quite annoyed.

It happens. In the throes of orgasm, you could mumble the name of your former mate. In a moment of anger or fear, you might call your new mate by an ex's name.

Some of us are good at suppressing our feelings, doubts, and concerns. Years pass. We are confident of being in control of the situation. Then we trip up. Ouch!

I think of "Glenda," married to a bonafide philistine womanizer. While she was in labor with their second child, he was with another woman. Eventually they divorced in a messy courtroom battle. Two years later she remarried, but *before* the wounds were healed.

Her former husband did not keep up with his child support payments. Then he died. Glenda was devastated by grief.

"Wait a minute!" her second husband demanded. "If he was that bad, why are you crying and carrying on like this?"

No matter what we may think or say, our first mate *still* has some territorial claims on our spirit.

Our first mate may have been amputated from our lives, our tax forms, and our photo albums, but not from our consciousness.

People regularly ask if I still love Jane. Yes, I do. But that love occupies a quiet corridor in my spirit. It's like a pan that has been placed on the back burner. Yet it's still there.

That does not mean that we will ever get back together. It simply means that you don't extinguish love 100%. Jane occupies a quiet place in my heart. She always will.

In time, many of the memories of Jane will fade. But I cannot ignore those six years of my life; nor do I want to. I have chosen to be selective: to remember the good things, like her hot cinnamon breakfast rolls. Why would I want to forget those?

Memories like that may be difficult for you. The mere mention of your ex's name may bring you pain. But in time, the positive memories will demand to be recognized and appreciated.

You may have to work through it with a counselor. Sometimes it may be a struggle. But memories do not have to be a menace. They can be a reminder that our brain takes seriously everything we say or do or feel or experience.

Take time to talk to your mate about those memories. Take time to live so that today's memories are jockeying for space with the old ones, literally crowding them out.

8   "I Wish My Children Understood"

Recently, in Los Angeles, two 90-year-olds stood before a judge, seeking a divorce.

"If you have lived together all these years, why are you seeking a divorce now?" the judge asked.

"We had to wait until the children died," was the reply.

At any age, a parents' divorce is tough to handle. Children's reactions to their parents' divorce(s) will depend on their ages and developmental levels.

The world of infants and toddlers is primarily focused around their mothers. They will react to any disruption in their mother's ability to respond to their needs, and may revert to earlier levels of development.

The world of preschoolers is often shattered by divorce. They may blame themselves. "If I had only been good. . . ."

Older children are less likely to assume responsibility. Instead, they may become angry or confused.

Teenagers, well on their way to adulthood, will struggle with new responsibilities, particularly for their younger brothers and sisters. They may feel torn between the two parents, who may attempt to win them over to their particular points of view.

Yet children quickly determine that they have to survive. They have remarkable resiliency.

As divorce has become more and more common, children have more peers to help them sort out their feelings.

Here are some suggestions:

- Be honest with your children.
- Quickly diffuse any hint of guilt on the part of your children for the divorce.

- Don't put down your ex in front of your children.
- Recognize the sphere of a child's questions. Most don't care who did what. Rather, they want to know, "What's going to happen to me?"
- Don't turn your children into undercover agents. Some parents use children to gather information about their exes.
- Be careful with promises.
- Remember a child's frame of reference. Suppose a parent says, "You're going to come and visit me." A four-year-old thinks, "I'd better get my coat." The parent could have meant in *two months*.
- Don't sneak around and hide your dating or social life from your children.
- Try not to disrupt too many areas of their lives. The more areas of change, the more confusion and frustration and anger.
- Help your children keep good memories alive.[1]

Children naturally will begin editing memories and then reviewing memories, looking for things to explain the divorce. Nicki Scott explained how some single parents try to crowd out "we/then" memories with "us/now" memories:

> Whenever they looked quiet or sad, I thought of another fun thing to do. I didn't want to hear how they felt—I was afraid their hurt would make me hurt even more. . . . Kids know; you can't fool them.[2]

Give your children the time and resources to talk through their grief. Many parents have found that child psychologists are particularly well-trained to facilitate such conversations.

Finally, it's important to realize that time heals wounds. Time may be the key element in softening the strain of a divorce on children.

9   *"I Wish My Parents Understood"*

The ripples of divorce reach far beyond the couple involved. Some of the most wounded are the parents and grandparents, particularly if this is the first divorce in a family. Suddenly, divorce is not what happens to "other" people but is happening to people with whom we share a last name and memories.

How a parent is told about a separation/ divorce is as crucial as the reality of what they are told.

Here are some common reactions parents have to the news of a divorce:

- *surprised:* "Why, I had no idea!"
- *suspected:* "Well, I thought something was wrong because . . . ."
- *expected:* "Doesn't surprise me a bit! I wondered how long it would last."
- *silence:* "I don't know what to say!"

For some parents, distance adds to the anguish. They feel frustrated and helpless. In some instances one parent keeps information from another.

Some people edit the reports they give of the decision in order to prevent a parent's premature response. "I'll kill him!" one father-in-law growled.

Some parents become angry that a son or daughter has not let them know that there were problems. And confusion comes when a son or daughter-in-law was well-liked. Parents then have ambivalent feelings; they are torn by their loyalty to *their* son or daughter and concern and love for the in-law.

In some instances, because of previous kiss-and-make-up episodes, parents are reluctant to accept the finality of a divorce.

Sooner or later parents have to be told. And one's first version of the story may have to be recalled if they are really to understand.

Some parents have immediate, negative reactions they may later regret. Others demand, "Where did I fail?" Many parents still view their grown children as extensions of themselves.

Others become embarrassed. "This reflects on us," one parent said sternly. Some want to pretend that it isn't happening. After all, many separations do not lead to divorce.

News of a divorce can be devastating to parents who have always been perceived as emotionally rock-solid. The one who always had the answers when the going got tough may suddenly be slow to respond or to reaffirm love.

Some parents are judgmental: "You got yourself into this mess. You'll have to get yourself out! I told you not to marry him (or her)!"

A few parents are like the cavalry charging up San Juan Hill. They want to be rescuers. They may think the solution to the problem is money and try to help that way—possibly with strings attached.

Finally, some parents want to declare martial law and resume active parenting. "Just leave everything to me," they say.

Some parents may not have objections to a divorce per se. However, 60% of divorced persons eventually remarry, and remarriage may present barriers for some parents on theological grounds.

If you do remarry, you will hopefully have had time to heal beforehand. But a parent may treat your prospective mate with hostility or coolness, particularly if there is a short engagement.

Some will resist because they are still holding out for a reconciliation. It may take time to win them over. I urge parents to ask three questions:

- What is this person really like?
- Can she or he help my son or daughter grow, mature, and heal?
- Am I erecting bridges or barricades?

And what about your former in-laws? Perhaps you enjoyed being with them. They may have laughed at your jokes, asked for seconds on your lasagna, and made you feel like a son or daughter. They may need time. No doubt they will feel confused and wounded. Some will be torn by their loyalties, particularly if there is a third party involved (who could now become an in-law).

Be kind. Be considerate.

Tragically, a few divorced people have almost had to divorce their parents. But most parents come through like troopers. Give them plenty of time and opportunities to understand.

10   *"I Wish Our Friends Understood"*

One thing about separation or divorce is that you soon discover who your real friends are.

Admittedly, a divorce can be hard on friends. For one thing, they will be struggling with the menacing accusation, "If it happend to *them*, it could happen to *us*." Sure, some friends will quickly discount such an idea, but the notion will come sneaking back. They will sift through scrapbooks, memories, and conversations, looking for clues to make sense of it all. Unfortunately, they may make outrageous assumptions in order to fit the pieces together.

Your divorce may actually be good for some of your friends because it will force them to deal with hairline cracks in their own relationships. Your trauma may dispel any of their fledgling longings for a divorce. You may succeed in making divorce a harsh reality for them rather than an abstract, potentially attractive option.

You may resent your ex. You may want to take him (or her) "to the cleaners." You may vow to make him or her "pay and pay dearly." But some of your friends will resist or even resent that attitude. Your friendship was a dual one, not a singular attraction. They liked both of you, and what will you say if you discover that your ex has already "won them over" or prejudiced them against *you*?

There are social realities to reckon with. Are they going to invite you over for coffee? for a meal? a night out? In some neighborhoods you may end up a social pariah. You simply won't be invited. After all, American society socializes in even numbers.

What if they invite your ex over? Will you give them latitude, or will you snarl across the back fence, "Whose side are you on, anyway?"

Some friends will work to get you back together. Jane had her birthday about a month after we separated. Our neighbors invited her for dinner, which was fine with me. But they also invited me over for dessert. "Would you like to come for cake and ice cream?" they asked.

I thought about the invitation. But I couldn't handle it. It was too hard to pretend everything was OK.

Some friends may betray you. They may—for a variety of reasons—share your confidences, take sides, or swap details with other friends.

One woman sent out notices to all her friends: "I am not in quarantine and I am not infectious!" After that her friends were more sociable.

The ultimate test of friendship may be a sexual "come on." Some will now disclose that their own marriage isn't so hot. Some may even offer to "service" you sexually.

"I couldn't believe it!" Mary Jane (later) laughed. "I mean, I didn't *want* to believe what I was hearing. Here was my best friend's husband, sitting at *my* kitchen table, talking mumbo-jumbo. Finally, I said, 'What exactly are you talking about?' He snickered, 'Do I have to spell it out?' Then he grabbed my hand and squeezed. 'I think you know.' "

"What happened then?" I asked.

"I sent him packing. And crossed them off my Christmas card list. But what really hurt was that he paused at the door and said, 'You'll change your mind.' "

It happens. It happens with the "best" of friends—friends who are supposed to understand, but who also know our vulnerability.

Perhaps, you argue, Mary Jane sent out mixed signals. Did she unintentionally lead him on? It's possible, but I doubt it.

How does one say good-bye to "our" friends? You mourn their loss, but you move on to new friends!

In many instances, saying good-bye to "our" friends will be a gradual loss rather than an amputation. You may suddenly realize that a year has passed and you haven't heard from them. Sometimes it won't make sense.

Be kind in judging their intentions. Fear makes friends do strange things. But remember that for every friend you lose, eventually you can gain a replacement.

11   *"I Wish Our Neighbors Understood"*

There is an old song by the title, "Wedding Bells Are Breaking Up That Old Gang of Mine." Some of your neighbors might well be humming, "Divorce is breaking up that old neighborhood of ours. . . ."

A divorce can be hard on a neighborhood. It used to be such a stigma that no one wanted to be the first on the block. Actually, it wasn't such a surprise in the days before air conditioning, when the windows were open for six months out of the year, and before the suburbs, when houses were built much closer together. People actually knew something (perhaps too much) about what went on next door. In those days neighbors used to talk over their fences at sundown. Now about all we do is wave. But the surprise factor has eroded. Very little really surprises us anymore.

Divorce is hard on neighbors because it's hard for them to put the puzzle pieces together. The "explainers" that they need are missing. Concerning recent arrivals, neighbors may say: "They *seemed* so happy." The divorces of old-timers are tougher to explain because there have been more shared experiences and more memories.

It's rough, frankly, because people realize that if it happened at *404* E. Laurelwood, it could happen at *402* or *406*.

A neighboring couple may not be equally attracted to each of you. So a divorce may mean the loss of one or both of them, especially if you have to sell the house. You may promise to get together or to keep in touch, but distance will make a difference. Besides, someone else will move into 404 E. Laurelwood and there will be a new link in the social circuit.

Neighbors range from nosy to merely observant. Suppose

there's an unfamiliar car in your driveway at 7:30 P.M. No big deal. But what if it's still there at 2:00 A.M. or 9:00 A.M.? That might stir up some gossip.

Some neighbors have been "burned" in the past by getting involved in domestic quarrels. The couple kissed and made up but then turned on the intruding neighbors. Such neighbors may now be reluctant to listen. This often happens in apartment complexes that have a high proportion of divorced people. "Live and let live" is the philosophy.

We need to face up to the fact that Americans have redefined the term *neighbor*. My grandfather participated in barn-raisings. If he finished his harvest early, he helped his neighbor. Borrowing things from neighbors gave us a chance to disclose tidbits which, when linked together, made sense. After all, you couldn't dash in and breathlessly demand, "Can I borrow a cup of sugar?" and then dash back out the door. You talked. Sometimes you stayed long enough for a cup of coffee. No longer do we go next door to borrow a cup of anything—that's what convenience stores are for.

Besides, many choose apartments and blend in. They don't take time to get to know their neighbors. After all, they're going to move when their six-month lease is up.

A friend of mine, Stephen Hicks, was annoyed to have someone banging on his door early one Monday morning:

> I swung open my apartment door. Standing before me was not a criminal, pervert or even a UPS man. But rather, a petite young lady with a slightly bewildered look on her face. . . . Before I could say anything more than hello she said, in somewhat halting English, that she had just moved into the apartment upstairs. Could she borrow my Yellow Pages?
>
> A little later she returned with the phone book. She shyly said that she didn't want to sit up in her apartment alone. Would I like to have a beer with her? . . . I simply said, "No thanks, I don't drink. But you're welcome to come down here while I have ice tea."

So there we were. Me with my ice tea and Sunny with her Coors. (I call her Sunny because I couldn't begin to spell or pronounce her Korean name.) In the next hour or so I learned that her life was anything but sunny. The wife of an American serviceman she met in Korea, her divorce had been final barely a week. She was now a woman and mother of three who was alone in the world without a job, the skills to get one, or even a family. She said it seemed like it would be winter in her heart forever.

I don't know what long-range plans God has for Sunny, or the part He may ask me to play in those plans. And it is a little scary to think He may ask me to lay down a part of my life so that He may begin to build His kingdom in Sunny's heart. *It may require more of me than simply loaning out my Yellow Pages or spending an hour in conversation. . . . My commitment should carry more weight than a two-pound phone book* [italics added].[3]

I think my friend Stephen found a new definition of the word *neighbor* that morning.

Give your neighbors every chance to understand. There may be a Stephen who will come through when you really need an ear, and in time you may be a Stephen to a neighbor.

---

12   "I Wish My Employer Understood"

Tennessee Ernie Ford popularized a folk song called "Sixteen Tons." The words are still potent:

Sixteen tons and what do you get?
Another day older and deeper in debt.
St. Peter, don't you call me,
   'cause I can't go.
I owe my soul to the company store.

One of the first questions many people ask when they are introduced to each other is, "What do you do?" Our jobs give us status or provide resources with which we can buy status. But does your boss understand?

No one knows the full effects of divorce on the workplace. Millions of hours of productivity are lost. Accidents happen because employees' minds are somewhere else. Many workers are so financially-strapped that they spend hours worrying about how to make ends meet. One recent study reported that divorced women and their children suffer an immediate 73% drop in their standard of living, while their ex-husbands enjoy a 42% rise in theirs.[4] Moreover, in the after-school hours, working single parents worry about the safety of their "latch-key" children.

Some divorced persons go to work knowing that no matter how hard they work, there will still not be enough money to go around. That leads to job dissatisfaction and depression. Others throw themselves into their work as if they were mindless zombies. It takes their minds off their personal stress.

Traditionally, employers have argued that the personal lives of employees are not relevant to their work. But today, with such a high percentage of the work force divorced or divorcing, managers are beginning to take another look. And as more managers and supervisors have become divorced, there has been more concern for the workers under them.

When a job comes first in a person's life, it can become a mistress. How many marriages have suffered because of jobs? How many workaholics have had trouble finding time for a divorce?

In a society that prizes upward mobility, many people are willing to sacrifice everything to get ahead. But once they achieve that goal they may not be able to enjoy it. Many people keep one eye on the next goal and the other looking over their shoulder to see who is behind them. Some have achieved their career goals only to find themselves alienated from their mates, children, and even coworkers.

How long will it be before someone sues a Fortune 500 company for "alienation of affection"?

What about your job performance right now? Some days you will simply not be able emotionally to be the model employee. You may not make your sales quota. Your boss may lean on you. There's still tomorrow.

Here are some guidelines for "surviving" your job during a divorce.

1. Talk to your supervisor. Fortunately, in most companies, the days are long passed when divorce implied "instability." However, there are realities that need to be discussed during the separation and initial recovery stage of your divorce. Many companies have employee assistance officers who are there to help you during this time. Take advantage of that assistance.

2. Don't drift into a workplace romance. The news about your separation/divorce may not make the company newsletter, but it will filter through the grapevine. Over coffee, you may find a fellow employee of the opposite sex more than willing to listen; some will be married, some divorced. If you are saying, "I wish someone understood," it's easy for someone to understand but misunderstand.

Some see you as sexually vulnerable; some may have problems in their own marriages. Be alert to your emotions. Remember that you will have to see them the next day at work.

3. Reevaluate your job. Why do you do what you do? Divorce can jar you into an objective evaluation of yourself. You may sense some of your untapped potential and develop new interests.

For some, divorce leads to promotions. They are free to move across the country, seemingly for a "fresh start." Others reject promotions so that they can remain close to their children.

4. Don't do anything hastily. It's easy for some workers to get down on themselves. "What's the use?" they ask. A few have decided to quit working as a way to get even with an ex. They may want to walk away from everything they have worked to build. It can be appealing to fantasize about that new start somewhere without old memories, but reality generally follows the moving van.

If you know you need change, plan carefully. Denis Waitley observed, "Planning is the bridge linking dreams and achievement."[5]

Finally, your job can be a way of refurbishing your wounded ego. Waitley says, "You are a Most Valuable Person in your work." My bet is that your company is glad to have you.[6]

If you are dreaming of real change, then look at your present job as a way of gathering resources to help you make that change.

You don't have to be the *best* employee. Just be a *good* employee who can be counted on.

---

13   *"I Wish My Pastor Understood"*

In times of stress, particularly marital stress, many people turn to the church and their pastor. There are a variety of responses encountered:

- privately sympathetic/publicly tolerant;
- privately sympathetic/publicly condemning;
- privately condemning/publicly condemning;
- privately tolerant/publicly neutral.

As early as 1815, Yale president Timothy Dwight taught, "It is incomparably better that individuals should suffer than that an Institution, which is the basis of all human good, should be shaken or endangered."[7]

Historically, the church has opposed divorce. However, in the late 1850s there emerged a new tolerance for divorce on the grounds of adultery. Because of the extent of venereal disease, thousands of wives had been infected by their unfaithful husbands.

In 1852, public debates on the issue were conducted in the *New York Tribune* by editor Horace Greeley. Henry James wrote,

> It is not essential to the honor of marriage that two persons should be compelled to live together when they hold the reciprocal relation of dog and cat, and that in the state of things divorce might profitably increase.[8]

Some ministers took a bolder course. In 1870, James G. Powers said, "There ought to be no human law to compel the continuance of any marriage, which, so long as it continues, is nothing better than legal prostitution."[9]

Today many religious leaders are caught in a squeeze: should they condemn divorce or condone it? Some choose a middle ground—silence.

Others have paraphrased Timothy Dwight's statement while debating the nuances of Matthew 19 in the Greek text. Meanwhile, church members hemorrhage emotionally.

Some churches have said *yes* to divorce but *no* to remarriage. That's half a loaf of bread to a starving person. That's theological fence-sitting.

Some congregations have instituted their own quasi-legal procedures to pinpoint a "guilty" party and an "innocent" party, the latter eligible to remarry with the blessing of the church.

Why are pastors reluctant to get involved?

1. Pastors are poorly trained as counselors. Most seminary educations allow little room for practical marriage and family courses. Students are too busy studying ancient languages or theology to study the language of marriage. Admittedly, many took the required course(s) in pastoral care, but that was a "cover-it-all in one semester" approach, from baptisms to burials.

2. Some pastors are not interested in counseling. One well-known pastor said, "You know, counseling is like taking a dipper to the ocean. You can spend all your time dipping with all your might, and when you are finished you haven't made much of a dent." [10]

3. Some pastors have weak egos and want to be messiahs of the emotions. They prefer dispensing platitudes on submission and how "you can work it out" to long-term counseling and grappling with real problems.

4. Many pastors are too busy to be effective counselors. Many pastors will agree to see any parishioner—once. Then they refer them to someone else. Some pastors are "fix-its" who say, "Here's my 1, 2, 3 approach." They want to solve your problem quickly because they have sermons to prepare, newsletters to edit, funds to raise, committees to chair, teas to attend, weddings to perform, etc. (Referring a parishioner to a more qualified counselor after about three visits, however, may not be a sign of being "too busy.")

5. Some pastors are not compassionate. To some degree, counseling is a skill that can be acquired. But the basic dynamics, such as listening and empathy, are gifts. Some pastors are teachers; some are preachers; only a few are counselors.

6. Some pastors have bad marriages. Clergy divorce has increased approximately 300% in the last decade.[11] One pastor confessed, "I am forced to take a hard line by my ecclesiastical superiors. But I've listened to many describe my own marriage in their words. I envy their freedom."

Many congregations have a double standard. Parishioners are expected to have problems but ministers are expected to be exemplars of family virtue. Some quickly find scriptural support in 1 Timothy to back up their expectations. Pastors who fail are defrocked or their careers hamstrung.

Many pastors are caught in a bind. They want to be compassionate and caring but they fear being labeled as "condoning" by their parishioners.

Give your pastor an opportunity. But remember, he or she has foibles and biases too.

Finally, if your pastor seems unable to offer the help you need, ask for a referral to a qualified counselor in your area.

Part Three

BARRIERS TO UNDERSTANDING

14 *The Editing Barrier*

You are reading at least the seventh draft of this chapter. First there was scribbling and rambling notes. Next came a rough pencil draft edited with a red pen. I added words and crossed out sentences. I polished the thoughts to make it flow better. Next came a typed copy, then more polishing. Eventually, my editor added his touch. Then I reworked it some more. Finally there were some last-minute changes by the editor.

**Whenever I edit my thoughts, I am
limiting your chance to understand.**

The same thing happens verbally. You see, I am often afraid for you to hear my raw thoughts. What would you think? So I edit.

When I was growing up, once in a while a teacher would threaten to call my dad because of my misconduct. On the way home from school, I would construct an "edited" version that skipped many "miscellaneous" facts. I didn't want to get my dad bogged down with a lot of details. Besides, my version put me in a better light. However, because of my editing, sometimes my dad was confused.

That's the problem with divorce. There are *always* two sides (and sometimes more). It's a tough task for judges, psychologists, and friends to sort through the facts and tales.

We have all made bad decisions and inherited the consequences. It's hard to be honest, to expose our inner selves to another person. Who can we trust? Even with a close friend it's hard to be honest. So we edit. We deny facts or details that might help others understand. We expect them to read between the lines.

Editing sabotages (or at least delays) understanding on the part of others. Can I really blame them for not understanding if I withhold essential information? In court you promise to "tell the truth—the whole truth and nothing but the truth." But that's in court.

Some editing may be necessary. For example, you can't tell a six-year-old everything or tell the story in the same way that you would tell an adult. Nor can you always tell everything to your parents, especially when there is the possibility of reconciliation. Some parents have incredible memories. And sometimes there are facts about your spouse that could ruin his or her career if they were known. So you edit.

Yet editing imposes a burden because some divorces don't add up. Some friends or family members will not be satisfied and will challenge your editing. They will want to know more. And it may not be appropriate to tell the whole story—except to a counselor in a confidential situation.

Some friends or family members can only take proportional segments. For example, the first draft of this book was too long, so it had to be edited and shortened. Some well-written paragraphs had to be deleted. That's hard on a writer, but it's also necessary for effective communication. Some of those paragraphs were side-roads that would have been too distracting for readers.

Editing is not lying. You may have the urge to say more, and others may misunderstand you. But that is part of the process.

Finally, you will need to be firm. Some friends have the tenacity of a bulldog or prosecuting attorney. They know how to word questions to elicit answers. A few may even badger, provoking your tears or anger. Will you give in? Now is the time to decide what your policy will be.

15   *The Silence Barrier*

"Silence is golden!"

"The less said the better."

Those two common clichés are the biggest roadblocks to communication. We're supposed to be able to "take it"—especially we males. And some women are drawn to the "strong, silent" types, but that works better on screen than in real life.

Some people seem to be able to endure great pain without complaint. General George Rogers Clark was such a man. In 1823 doctors had to amputate his leg. In those days of primitive surgery, whiskey was the only anesthetic. As the surgeon began, up marched the army regimental band. During the entire operation the band played. General Clark tapped his fingers to the tune and beat. That's courage.

Oh, but not everyone can be that strong.

Scripture says, "as a lamb before the shearer is silent, so he did not open his mouth" (Acts 8:32, referring to Jesus). As much as I admire Jesus, I cannot be that courageous. I want to moan, wail, and pour out my complaint.

What promotes silence?

- *Martyrdom.* Some people want to be heroes. So divorce becomes the latest arena in which to demonstrate strength and reserve.
- *Lack of trust.* Once they trusted someone, and that person "talked." Now they resist putting their confidence in others.
- *Lack of confidence.* They doubt that talking will change anything. "What good does it do to talk about it?"
- *Lack of experience.* Some people have never talked about personal matters. They are victims of traditions that may have been in their family for generations. Or they may be afraid of saying something that sounds "dumb." So they say nothing.
- *Desire to protect the ex.* Many still love an ex, perhaps hoping for a reconciliation. So "the less said the better."
- *Lack of discretion.* These people do not have "control." They are indiscriminate. Any ear will do. And they may barter information. You tell *me* something and I'll tell *you* something.

Remember that quip, "O Lord, help my words to be nutritious, in case I have to eat them."

"Motor-mouths" wear down potential listeners and helpers. No wonder people duck when they see them coming. Some discretion and periods of silence might be valuable.

But silence can become a wall—the ultimate barricade. Robert Louis Stevenson observed, "The cruelest lies are often told in silence."

16   The Uniqueness Barrier

After reading my book *Jason Loves Jane but They Got a Divorce,* many people have told me, "That could have been Bill Loves Susan (Debbie Loves Stephen, etc.)—my story."

There is something universal about the experience of divorce that causes people to identify with another's story. This is why divorce recovery and support groups are so valuable. They provide a place where we can be understood. Janet Nelson explained, "I finally had a language I could use so that someone else could understand . . . what had been a very important and yet painful experience." Moreover, "I had arrived in the ring that was large enough for most of the questions that interested me to be answered."[1]

Yet some divorced people ignore resources right in their own zip code, arguing, "My situation is different." This attitude is more pride than anything else. It translates into, *"My* divorce is worse than *yours."*

In all divorces, there are common threads.

I maintain that if we look for what we have in common we will find a closeness to anyone experiencing a divorce. Maybe one divorce is simpler or less complicated, depending on finances, length of marriage, number of children, etc.

But remember this: you are a unique person going through a tough situation. You need to find ways to use that uniqueness to help you survive and to help you reach out to others. Otherwise your uniqueness becomes suffocating, an impossible burden.

Sometimes what passes for "uniqueness" is camouflage. This is a problem for those who have bisexual or homosexual mates.

Suppose you tell "all." He could lose his job, and you've got two kids to support.

The wife of one of my friends became involved with a religious celebrity. "I never told anyone," my friend said, "because it would have destroyed another marriage. So I kept it to myself."

Don't allow your perception of your "uniqueness" to keep you from finding help through counseling and support groups. What you thought was "unique" might be more common than you had imagined.

---

17   *The Martyrdom Barrier*

Computers have incredible capacity to store data and recall it in microseconds. But so does your mind. In his book *Overcoming Depression,* Paul Hauck wrote:

> You are going to have to learn (if you want to avoid depression) that while you are living on the face of this earth, unfair and unkind behavior in exchange for your loving efforts *is the rule* rather than the exception. The sooner you realize that things will always be that way, the healthier you will become.[2]

One of the favorite phrases or clichés of the divorced is, "It isn't fair." But who said life had to be fair? How many of us have formulated a system like this:

"If I do X, then I should receive _____ ."

"If I do Y, then I should receive _____ ."

But as soon as the system seems to work, life says, "Oh yeah? Watch this!"

Injustice is a reality. I've seen sports enthusiasts scream, riot, and threaten mayhem because of a referee's call. We like to see a baseball manager charge out onto the field, protesting an umpire's call. The more the manager rants and raves, the more we scream, "You tell 'em!" It's a great drama on a hot summer night.

The notion that bad things shouldn't happen to good people is a strong one. Yet reality often interferes with our fantasies and notions.

Perhaps you've moved to a new neighborhood, taken a new job, and discovered that things have a way of following you.

Mabel became severely depressed after her 28-year-marriage ended. Another woman was involved. Her husband got off with a light financial settlement: no alimony. At first she was angry at him. Later she became angry at a legal system that ignored her needs. Eventually that anger turned into depression. The system and also many of her friends ignored her pain.

Such tragedies can lead either to depression or to revenge. Joseph Kennedy told his sons, "Don't get mad—get even!" Yet all of us have faced circumstances that we couldn't change.

That's the danger of file cards, those 3″ x 5″ cards in the metal or plastic boxes. When someone wrongs us we reach for a card and record the details, mumbling, "One of these days you'll get yours!"

Eventually the weight of so many cards wears us down. Many libraries still use card catalogs to list the books they have. One individual file card doesn't weigh that much. But the larger the library, the larger the card catalog. Considering that each book has at least three cards, suddenly you have a lot of weight.

"But it isn't fair!" you may protest. That may be true, but file cards can destroy you. The apostle Paul had good reason to say that love "keeps no record of wrongs" (1 Cor. 13:5). The desire to get even only keeps the wound fresh and delays healing.

Sometimes you need to surrender your cards—all your claim

checks. It's the best gift we can give ourselves. You can reduce your depression and despair by just tearing them up.

Do yourself a favor—don't be a martyr!

Love keeps no record of wrongs, but angry people keep their records up-to-date and up-to-the-minute. Nothing gets by them. The choice to end your martyrdom may require one courageous act: to tear up the cards.

18   The Shame Barrier

- "I am so embarrassed. . . ."
- "Divorce doesn't happen in *our* family!"

Divorce can trigger intense memories of shame from your childhood. Do you remember a parent demanding, "Aren't you ashamed of yourself?" or "I'd be ashamed if I were you!" Often these statements from years ago hurt because they were applied in situations in which we had little control. Your parents may not actually have verbalized such thoughts, but there were probably times when you suspected they were thinking them.

Over the years, shame has been widely used as a control or manipulative technique. Families stayed together "for the sake of the children," which really meant to avoid the shame and stigma. What guilt that dumped on children! Arrangements such as separate bedrooms and limited accountability allowed parents to maintain a good "public" image.

One young woman was surprised when she went home at Christmas. Eighteen months earlier she had married a college basketball player. But she had now been divorced for three months. People at her home church kept asking, "Where's Bill?"

"In Kansas City," she responded, hesitantly. (How could she know for sure?) On Sunday the pastor who had married them saw her in church. "Say," he grinned, "where's that man of yours?" Margie's eyes darted to her mother, who stared down at the floor. Margie had the distinct impression that the pastor didn't know that she was divorced.

"I'll be in the car!" she said to her mother and slipped out the door.

Later, on the way home, Margie's mother said, "I was so embarrassed, I didn't tell anyone!" Margie did not stay for Christmas.

How much stigma can you endure, particularly if you "inherited" the divorce? Contrary to the opinion held by so many undivorced people, it does not take two to tango. In most states, even if one party objects, the divorce will still be granted.

Shame also influences our gullibility. We're not embarrassed at the divorce per se, but by our naiveté. We say, "Everyone knew except me!" or "I was the last one to know!" We're not anxious to admit that our marriage failed. And we don't want to admit that we were not aware of a mate's infidelity (particularly if it was long-term).

Beth was married seven years to a practicing homosexual, but was devastated when he was arrested in a public restroom on a sex solicitation charge. Then she discovered that his sexual preference had been common knowledge. "You must have been pretty dumb not to have known," one of her friends chided.

"Well, I was naive," she answered. "I grew up in a small town. He was the only man I dated. How was I to know?"

Before you let shame harass you, ask yourself a few questions:

- Is this shame or pseudo-shame?

- Do I really have anything to feel ashamed about?
- If yes—what can I do about it?
- If no—what do I do about it?

A few people will prophesy all sorts of dire woes that are certain to befall you if you persist in this separation or divorce:

- "Your kids will turn out bad!"
- "You'll find out that men won't date you if you don't sleep with them!"

Stigmas wound and hurt. But ultimately, *you* decide their effect on you.

Life is waiting to give you the opportunity to prove your critics wrong.

---

19 The Pride Barrier

"I can do it myself" is a common cliché for two-year-olds and for many divorced people (though the latter often use more exclamation marks).

Pride becomes a barrier when we refuse to accept the gifts of love, affirmation, and acceptance that exist in our own zip code—when we insist on shouting, "No one understands!" What fuels pride?

- *Family experience.* Some of us come from families that teach nonreliance on others. Self-sufficiency is prized. That way you won't be disappointed if others don't come through.

● *Determination to prove something.* Remember the doom-sayers? Their prophesies and jeremiads of doom, despair, and misery still echo in your spirit. So you decided to prove everyone wrong, including your ex. You said, "I'll show 'em!" But will you lose the war as you try to win some obscure battle? It is a fatal mistake to let individuals barb us into such defensiveness.

● *Anger.* Perhaps you've approached someone for help, for a listening ear. They failed you. Or they talked. Now you snarl, "Who needs them?" *You* do!

● *Fear of provoking commentary.* Some people have unfinished emotional agendas. Don, for example, is afraid to ask his parents for money. He assumes that his father will say, "Didn't I *tell* you not to marry her?" Don's parents could easily help him, but he fears their editorializing. "I just don't need that," he moans.

"But you need the money," I counter.

"Yes, but not that badly."

After some time has elapsed, divorced people are glad they had some measure of pride and self-worth. "I have the satisfaction of knowing that I survived this." Maybe you can skip meals, go hungry, or not buy clothes this season. However, if there are children involved, you may have to surrender some of your pride for their benefit.

Some parents rationalize that the assistance they give their divorced son or daughter is for their grandchildren. One man even makes out checks to his grandchildren rather than to his daughter.

Pride has been a barrier to reconciliation—whether it be re-marriage or harmony between parents of the same child. "Let her crawl," said Stan, a 37-year-old truck driver. "Oh, but Stan," I prodded, "Is that for your best benefit or so that you won't lose face with your buddies who talked you into being hard-nosed with her?"

Sometimes pride keeps us from admitting how broke we are. It forces us to construct excuses of why we can't do something. But it also promotes creative shortcutting.

Your pride may be a barrier for others. For example, many married people assume that because a court has ordered or awarded child-support or alimony, you collect it. Yet each year, 50% goes uncollected. As a result of pride, some will not use existing channels to prod the collections. One friend of mine even suggested getting the Mafia involved. "I'd be willing to give them 50 cents on the dollar of everything they collect!" she laughed.

Many men have gotten away with shirking their responsibilities by the collective pride of women—women whose "belt-tightening" is motivated more by pride than skill.

There are people who want to help you. But don't let pride stand in the way. Tell them. Give them some ideas on how they could help.

Janice talked about the stigma of becoming a welfare mother. "I felt such a disgrace until I decided that I had paid my dues into the system. So I was merely withdrawing what I had paid. I didn't call it welfare or public assistance anymore. And I held each check and vowed, 'Someday I won't need you anymore.' "

**Pride must be balanced and prudent.
Pride has led some people to delay seeking
assistance until the easy, simpler solutions
and remedies were no longer available.**

By the third missed payment it may be too late to catch up.

Asking is not the same thing as demanding. Don't let pride keep you from creative solutions.

Part Four

DEALING WITH FEARS

20   The Fear Landscape

"I sought the Lord, and he answered me; he delivered me from all my fears" (Ps. 34:4).

It is a hot, hot, summer day. Notice the small boy, sitting on the edge of the swimming pool, watching. Watching other children diving off the diving board. Wishing he could. Oh, he's thought a lot about it. "Someday," he whispers to himself, wishing it could be today.

Perhaps, if no one were around, he would try. He knows what to do. Walk down the sidewalk, climb up the ladder, walk out on the board, bounce, then jump! Enjoy. Repeat until exhausted.

Yet something keeps him glued to the side of the pool. Fear.

Fear is the great spoiler. It's like acid, spilled on cloth. It destroys. Yet the wish, the desire, remains. Sometimes, the more intense the fear and the more dazzling the dream, the more accusing the "if onlys."

Fear produces depression. The distance between the dream and reality is fear's turf. It is a vigorous tug-of-war confined to the playground of your mind.

Several common fears taunt the divorced:

- fear of rejection
- fear of success
- fear of change
- fear of growing old
- fear of becoming ill
- fear of hormones
- fear of the stigma
- fear of being poor
- fear of myself
- fear of the system

Fear pushes you back into the rut of habits—sometimes rather roughly. Some of us claw our way to the top and catch a whiff of our dream. Then we hear the taunts.

It is good to have available for some other emotion the space that fear takes up in our lives.

That was the experience of the Israelites. Every morning the giant, Goliath, would come out and bellow, "I defy the ranks of Israel! Give me a man and let us fight each other" (1 Sam. 17:10). The Israelites had an acute shortage of courage and volunteers, to say the least.

The result was collective depression. "On hearing the Philistine's words, *Saul and all the Israelites* were dismayed and terrified" (v. 11, italics added). That translates into *depressed*. His haranguing continued for 40 days and 40 nights. Each day the depression grew darker—until a delivery boy, David, dared ask, "Who is this uncircumcised Philistine that he should defy the

armies of the living God?'' (1 Sam. 17:26). That question provoked his brother Eliab's wrath. Depressed people can be edgy.
Few of us want anyone to belittle our fear.

Yet David killed Goliath. David's courage sparked a major
Israelite offensive and earned David a niche on the Jewish hit
parade. "The women came out from all the towns of Israel to
meet King Saul with singing and dancing. . . . they sang, 'Saul
has slain his thousands. . . .' ''

Can you see King Saul beaming? Then the women sang verse
two: " '. . . *and David his tens of thousands*' '' (italics added).
What? Saul was outraged by the lyrics. "This refrain galled him''
(1 Sam. 18:6-8).

Let's analyze this story. The three men—David, Eliab, and
Saul— all had two common enemies: Goliath and their fear. Only
David chose to face down the fear, and he thereby eliminated
both it and the giant.

David's action created a personal reaction in the other two.
They replaced their fear of Goliath with resentment for David.

The fear of divorce—of change—taunts a lot of people. "What
if . . .'' threatens them. Some will secretly admit, "I wish I had
the courage to leave,'' but no sooner are those words spoken than
guilt arrives. "Marriage is forever! For better or worse!''

You may have had to face down your fears about survival to
file for a divorce. Your action threatens some friends, so your
decision will gall them. Some will respond with snide, caustic
remarks—words that will wound you.

What do you do about your fear?

1. Face it. Stare it down. Don't cower. Some fear is normal.
But excessive fear sabotages the possibilities for growth and survival.

2. Don't nourish it. Some divorced people with active imag-
inations rehearse mentally all the "terrible, horrible, no good''
things that *could* happen. They could get robbed, or raped, or
mugged, or become seriously ill. Yes, those things *could* happen.
But these things can happen to married people too.

3. Celebrate your inner strengths. You are special, one of a kind. Don't let fear keep you "dry," like the boy looking at the diving board. Dive into your fears and watch them give way.

4. Evict fear. Fear is always a pushy and selfish houseguest. It finds nice, "comfy" places in our lives where it makes itself at home. Evict fear and make room for growth. Go back and reread the growth principle on p. 57. Now what about your fears? What are you going to do to evict them?

Fear is a choice. Fear can incapacitate you—even paralyze you—so that you cannot respond to the circumstances you are facing today. But fear functions best with your permission and cooperation.

The alternative I recommend is to fight the first seeds of fear with an antidote of reality. By fighting your fear(s), you give yourself permission to live triumphantly and successfully despite your circumstances.

Fear is a choice.

21   Fear of Myself

"What makes you think that you . . . ?" is a common cliché, often heard from those who claim to love us the most. At age 17, I volunteered to direct our church's Christmas pageant. I can still hear my mother's protest: "What makes you think that you can do that?"

"I can do it," was my answer then, and now. I've never feared myself. I've sensed that within me is some spark of potential that, when properly directed, can be spectacular. Recognizing that is not arrogance on my part. I believe you could say the same thing about yourself.

First-person singular fear is disastrous.

● How many stay in dead, even violent marriages because they are more afraid of themselves than they are of their spouses?

● How many stay in the bargain basement of sleazy sexual relationships because they are afraid of a second marriage?

● How many blitz their minds with TV and noise because they fear silence?

● How many are "dating addicts," afraid of being alone with themselves?

Well, that's kind of abstract. Let's get personal.

● Do you fear that you might not only survive but thrive (and thereby prove too many people wrong)?

● Do you fear that you might do more than simply respond to this test of courage?

● Do you fear that your best might not be enough to see you through?

● Do you fear that you might prove your ex wrong?

● Do you fear that you might not be able to control yourself?

● What is it that stokes your fear? Certainly you weren't born with it. Have you allowed someone or something to water those seedlings of doubt that you have accumulated?

You are the perfect gift to yourself and perhaps, in time, to another.

In the meantime, I dare you:

—to give yourself some credit;

—to give yourself some room;

—to give yourself to yourself;

—to give yourself to your family;

—to give yourself to a church;

—to give yourself to a cause bigger than you are.

You are a precious resource that is too valuable to be wasted.

If you are challenged and are able to "get your act together," you might:

- write a perfect poem;
- write the next best-seller;
- compose the next hit;
- make a great scientific breakthrough;
- be a humanitarian who makes a contribution to world peace;
- invent the next "wheel."

Someone today is looking for that special product of your imagination—your creativity.

Fear of yourself can be your most relentless enemy.

---

22   *Fear of Change*

"Nothing endures . . . but change," said Heraclitus. "All is flux, nothing stays still." If that was true in the fifth century B.C., how much more true it is today.

There are three types of change faced by a divorced person:

- *chaotic*—one party moves out in the middle of a raging argument. No hint or warning: bang!
- *therapeutic*—undertaken as a deliberate and *joint* attempt to prevent further mutual hurt.[1]
- *selfish*—one party stuns the other by planning the exit to meet his or her own needs.

Any of these types of change can hurt. Bob Benson wrote that this generation is "engrossed in somehow trying to make the present permanent."[2] How many have said, "Just when I thought we had it made," or, "Just when I thought that was all behind us," he or she left.

In some ways things are easier on the one who initiated or planned the separation, or who has a new person on the side to "smother" the pain, confusion, or second thoughts.

If you cannot at this point see any pattern to what is happening, eventually you will. Wayne Oates has described the path of change in a marriage relationship as "the private rituals":

1. The husband and wife cease to keep track of one another.
2. The husband and wife cease to reach out to each other in time of need. They "go it alone."
3. The husband and wife cease to touch each other, to caress each other, to want to be near each other (although there may still be "public displays").
4. The husband and wife quit having sexual relations with each other; they quit sleeping in the same bed or room.
5. The couple ceases to live under the same roof.
6. The couple ceases.[3]

Rarely does anyone not go through at least several of these stages en route to the gavel.

However, there is a problem here. Divorce is one of the few rites of passage in our society that has not been institutionalized—although with "divorce" cards from Hallmark, we're getting closer. Doug Kimmel points out that such a recognition makes it easier because "the new roles are not prescribed by social norms. Instead, one has to formulate all these new roles (and reexamine the old ones) with little outside support and with almost no normative guidelines."[4]

Some of us are too busy yelling, "Make it stop hurting *now!*" Sometimes, when the ball is rolling, it is hard to stop.

Tragically, many divorces are triggered by someone running

from something. That's the particular tragedy of "mid-life crisis" divorces in which the man throws out the baby, the bathwater, and the bathtub as well.

All of us have a tendency to resist change. Buckminster Fuller suggested, "Change the environment; do not try to change man." Tens of thousands of mates have concluded, "My ex will never change," and have decided to change their environment.

Carolyn Koons, director of the Center for Creative Change at Azusa Pacific University, has identified four things that occur with change. Basically these are the "risks" of change. You have to:

- give up the familiar things (which is tough for the security-conscious);
- move into unknown areas;
- run the risk of criticism;
- run the risk of self-discovery.

Change brings growth, because of the interaction of the first four.[5]

You cannot get off the roller-coaster of change halfway through. Once you start, you ride to the end.

Even though you may resist change at first, you *can* survive it. I suspect that deep inside, you already know that.

23   *Fear of Losing My Children*

"I thought that if I was the perfect father, my children would grow up to call me blessed," says one single parent, "but they call me *collect*!"

Many children are caught in an emotional tug-of-war between two warring parents. Yet many single parents say, "I don't know what I would do without my kids." Indeed, we now have thousands of "kidnapped" children—kidnapped by the noncustodial parent. Too many parents forget that the problem is between two ex-spouses, not between two adults who have a child in common.

Instead of concentrating on the question of physical custody, I want to focus on how to avoid losing the *confidence* of your children.

1. Don't try to be both parents to your children. One good parent is better than two bad parents.

2. Be the parent that you are. Don't try to be a buddy or a pal.

3. Accept your limitations. You cannot get it all done. Do what you can. Dave Stoner reminds single parents that having dishes in the sink is not a sign of moral perversion.

4. Learn to nurture yourself. You need time to breathe. Children who have already lost one parent cannot afford to lose a second one.

5. Let the child be a child. A child is not a pseudo-adult or quasi-mate. A boy cannot be "momma's little man." He is a boy.

Catherine J. Blusiewicz, a counselor in Atlanta, works with many single parents and is concerned about child depression. "They've got the same worried look their parents have. They're like little, miniature adults. I get 9- and 10-year-olds coming in who talk about the light bill, the rent's due."[6]

One should also be hesitant to involve children in "the games" of single parenting, identified by Alice Peppler in her fine book, *Single Again: This Time with Children.*[7] Some of these are sure-fire ways to lose a child's respect and confidence.

- I SPY   I want to know about . . .
- LET MERCURY DO IT   Children pass on information we'd
                              rather not

• POISON BUTTON	One parent verbally puts down the other parent
• LOOK WHAT HE/SHE MADE ME DO	blaming the other parent for one's personal failures
• SANTA CLAUS	buying or reassuring through gifts
• KEEP AWAY	keeping data from one parent
• LET'S PRETEND	parent pretends child is substitute mate or friend

The Foundation for Children with Learning Disabilities has produced an excellent standard on childhood: "Let no child be demeaned, nor have his wonder diminished, because of our ignorance or inactivity. Let no child be deprived of discovery, because we lack the resources. Let no child ever doubt himself or his mind because he is unsure of our commitment."[8]

Remember, thousands of people have been good single parents: look at Mrs. Namath's boy "Joe" and Mrs. Wilson's son, Woody.

Are you a candidate for burnout as a single parent?

Do you:

- feel irreplaceable as a parent?
- dread weekends?
- suffer from colds, lower back pain, or insomnia?
- wish your kids would leave you alone?
- take drugs, drink, or overeat to hold down anger?
- feel that your children don't appreciate you?
- feel powerless to make a difference with your children?

If you answered yes to several of the above, then according to Joseph Procaccini and Mark Kiefaber, you may be headed for parental burnout.

In their book *Parent Burnout,* they list unreasonable expectations on the part of parents who:

- focus all their attention on the children;
- feel irreplaceable as a parent;
- cannot stand the thought of being an "average" parent;
- judge themselves by the successes of their children;

- deny their own needs for rest and recreation;
- live in fear of being disgraced by some act of their children;
- set unrealistically high standards for daily and lifetime accomplishments;
- feel the need to "corner the market" on the child's devotion;
- are unable to say no to demands from children or exes;
- focus negatively on the past: "If only we had . . .";
- create worries about the future: "What will happen if . . . ."[9]

Maybe you need to take time out to put your feet up or draw a hot tub of water. Then read this prayer:

Lord, grant me

time enough
to do all the chores,
join in all the games,
help with the lessons, and say night prayers,
and still have a few minutes left over for me;

energy enough
to be a bread baker and bread winner,
knee patcher and peacemaker,
ball player and bill juggler;

hands enough
to wipe away the tears,
to reach out when I'm needed,
to hold and to hug,
to tickle and to touch;

heart enough
to share and to care, to listen and to understand,
and to make a loving home
for my family.

—anonymous

To this I would add, "simply to be a good enough parent to make a difference in the life of my children."

24   *Fear of Losing My Friends*

It's easy for divorced persons to believe their friends are abandoning them or talking about them.

Some people avoid divorced people. Occasionally, there are good reasons for it. Some may think, "It could be *me*!" That's a troubling thought. They will do anything to avoid the suggestion.

Friendship is, after all, a two-way street. In order to have friends you have to have planted "friend seeds." Have you put your eggs in too few baskets, so that when you *need* a friend none is available? "But I need a friend *now*" whined Sheila. But friendships are like money in a bank account. Before you can withdraw you have to have deposited.

Sheila doubted her friends' sensitivity.

"They're talking about me—behind my back!" she scowled.

"How do you know?"

"I can tell!" she snapped.

Admittedly, some may be *talking,* but that is not necessarily gossiping. To some of your friends, your divorce is like a jigsaw puzzle. Some of the pieces are missing. So they exchange impressions, express their concern, and discuss how they can help you. Sometimes, through such conversations, someone gives someone else an idea of something they can do to help you.

So the next time you're tempted to conclude that your friends are abandoning you, give it a second thought. Is that *really* true? Or are you using self-pitying self-talk? Are you bearing false witness against your friends?

"No one cares" is a dramatic-sounding statement. But is the statement *really* true? If "no one cares," why did Christ suffer and die? His death invalidates your statement. For if just one person cares, then your words aren't accurate.

Admittedly, not everyone will respond *as you wish*. Not everyone will drop everything and come running to help you. But it is possible to become so wrapped up in your own pain that you don't hear the pain of others.

In one hospital experiment a severely depressed woman was placed in a ward with 10 other patients. Because of financial cutbacks, there was inadequate staff for the patients. So this woman began reaching out to others: carrying food trays, brushing hair, comforting. Her actions prompted a change in that ward. In a short time she had touched the lives of many people and recovered from her own depression. Reaching out to others could have the same effect on you.

Ironically, our "nobody cares" attitudes may keep people at a distance. They are afraid to invade our territory. "Nobody cares" sounds like, "Keep out! Trespassers will be shot!" Sometimes we reject the very resources God intended to use to bring healing and comfort to us.

Some days *you* have to lower the drawbridge in order to let your friends in!

But suppose you're right. They *are* talking. Is that the end of the world? No! The absence of an old friend makes room for a new friend. Sometimes a forest must be thinned out to make room for new trees.

Sometimes we have to say good-bye to friends.

But don't be too hasty. Friendships stretch and strain, but most endure. You may be surprised to find that in this low time there will be new proof of the strength of your friendships.

Give your friends time and space. Always leave the door slightly ajar. They may fear *your* rejection, too. But share your feelings with them. Otherwise they will never know.

Give them some hints of how they might help you.
Be "invadeable."

---

25   *Fear of Rejection*

Rejection is unpleasant. I know. As a writer, I have collected
more than my share of rejection slips. There's rarely such a thing
as a good rejection. I try to avoid the experience as much as
possible.

Maybe you got several dump-truck loads of "you-talk" in the
process of divorce. Your ex may occasionally restock your supply.

One of my friends was remarried several years after her divorce, to a very fine man. They loved to exchange notes: on
pillows, in lunch bags, on the kitchen counter. Sometimes the
notes were syrupy, sometimes sensual.

One day Pat came home and found a note on the kitchen table.
It read, "Don't take this personally . . . but I'm leaving you."
It took several minutes for her to realize this wasn't a joke. *Don't
take it personally?*

In my own case, my ex's parting words were, "You're a great
guy *but*. . . ." Great comment after six years.

Hopefully your divorce is a rejection of the relationship, not
of you. Some exes become good friends once the marriage is
over.

Indeed, some marriage scholars argue that divorce is not a
rejection of the institution of marriage. They cite as evidence the
high rate of rapid second marriages. Divorce is usually a rejection
of a relationship with a particular person.

At any rate, you are probably now divorced. The real tragedy of this experience is that significant numbers of people snarl,

—"Never again!"

—"All men (or women) are alike!"

Future relationships are therefore limited by fear (real or imagined) of a second rejection.

Yes, the divorce rate among those who marry a second time is also high. But why? I don't think it's because of remarriage per se, but because *(a)* a lack of healing time; and *(b)* a lack of patience and risk-taking. We boast, "I learned my lesson the hard way." But a riskless life is so boring!

You may be considering a live-in relationship or a "marital audition." Lawrence Kurdick's study of 188 couples found that a high percentage of those living together viewed their relationship as experimental. They tended to be divorced, "very cautious, very pragmatic, somewhat unromantic. They have *chosen* not to marry." [10]

So they play house instead. "We're together *until* something (or someone) splits us up."

Dr. Ray Short has studied live-ins extensively, and has noted that

> . . . most of the males see the living-in as an alternative to, and not a preparation for, marriage. If the subject of marriage comes up, they either lie or hedge. They say to her such things as, 'The time isn't right yet' or 'I'm just not ready to settle down.' *In fact they have no intention at all of ever marrying their partner* [italics added]. . . . if he told her the truth he'd likely lose his warm bed." [11]

Counselors are now seeing just about as many broken, mangled hearts from live-in relationships as from marriage. Short concluded, "A broken heart hurts just as much from a live-in breakup as from any other kind." [12]

You can't enjoy the good life while you are afraid of getting hurt.

Prudent caution is advisable, but compulsive caution is not.

What if Ronald Reagan had sworn, "Never again!" after his divorce from Jane Wyman? What if he had chosen to filter his future through the lens of rejection?

If you really want to avoid rejection, consider the sage advice of Bud and Kathy Pearson found in *Single Again: Remarrying for the Right Reasons:* "Love is a decision, *not a feeling*." They urge you to:

- check out spiritual values;
- check out attitudes;
- check out interests;
- check out habits;
- check out life-style.[13]

If you give yourself time to heal and check out the basics, that fear of rejection will fade from view and you will experience love again. And your example may encourage another divorced person.

26 Fear of Damnation

Once upon a time the church had incredible power over all aspects of people's lives, because people believed the church possessed the keys to eternal life.

Thousands of Catholics and Protestants stayed in loveless marriages because if they divorced they would be publicly disciplined or excommunicated. If they should die in such a lapsed state of grace. . . . well, everyone understood the consequences.

Some stayed; some strayed. Others paced their homes with the fury of a caged tiger. Others formed "arrangements" that tolerated marital freedom and, at times, an affair.

That same system forced people into vow-making at ages when they were much too immature to understand the nuances of "for better or for worse." Some of those forced marriages were funerals for people's dreams. But they stayed in relationships as the last vestiges of their dreams were squeezed out of them. Some found solace in alcohol or one-night stands—mostly momentary respites from the tension and loneliness.

The Catholic tradition prohibited people from using most forms of contraception. Sex was seen as only a procreative activity. Along came another child, often too soon after the last one. More resentment.

How many mangled husbands and wives coveted the independence of a son or daughter who refused to buy into the old system? How many breathed easier—yet guiltily—when their life partner died prematurely? How many have remarried, found how good marriage can be, and now curse the tortuous, painful years?

How many desperately sought freedom? "Anything has to be better than this!" How many wondered how a loving God could eternally punish them for a longing for "more"?

Whatever happened to hell? We used to have "hellfire and damnation" preachers in pulpits, not just on television on Sunday mornings. At some point this nation underwent a theological change. The demise of preaching about hell was joined by a new view of God and also a new perspective on marriage.

Still, there are those who fear damnation. Andrew Greeley described it well in *The Cardinal Sins,* where one priest observed, "I could hear the despair of a man who had been in a cave so long he would never recognize the light again."[14]

**As long as we enter marriage so
frivolously, so foolishly, at hormonal
floodtide, there will be a high divorce rate.**

Yet God wants to create order out of chaos. Out of the dark voids of our own lives God works to bring peace. We were wrong about God for so many years. We blasphemed him by making him a doting old grandfather with snow-white hair, a bloodthirsty accountant-tyrant, or an intruding meddler.

Yet the God whom so many fear is the same God who would so willingly give his Son to redeem a bunch of failures. His Son passed over the opportunity to condemn a woman divorced not once, but divorced five times (John 4). Jesus saw beyond her sin and recognized her potential.

Rather than condemn her, Jesus pointed her to a new freedom, to the possibility of becoming the person her Creator dreamed she could be. Jesus freed her from all who would condemn her.

"Go to hell!" is a too-commonly used exclamation among the divorced, who hurl it at someone they once claimed to love.

People who threaten dire eternal consequences to the divorced have to overlook the words of Jesus as well as those of Paul. Jesus asked the woman caught in adultery where her accusers had gone (John 8:10). They had disappeared! And the simple beauty of God's grace is found in Paul's statement, "Therefore, there is now no condemnation for those who are in Christ Jesus" (Rom. 8:1).

Freedom scares so many people.

For 250 years, Christians have sung these words of Charles Wesley:

He breaks the power of cancelled sin;
He sets the prisoner free.
His grace can make the foulest clean
His grace availed for me.

27   *Fear of Not Surviving*

Suppose you prove them all wrong? You know—the ones who told you:

—your kids would end up turning against you;

—you'd lose your home to foreclosure.

I'm not sure how long it takes to "prove it" to some people. No doubt, a few will remain obstinate and refuse to soften their prophecies. Surely, some will be surprised, and a few will be disappointed that you didn't end up the way they said you would.

It's often hard to accept the fact that you are breaking your wedding vows. Some people fear the stigma of "breaking the vows." Yet, as I pointed out in *Warm Reflections,* "vows made at a flower-lined altar are only as good as those made at the altar of the heart daily." Usually by the time people fear breaking their vows, they have already long been broken.

Many have chosen to live under the sword of Damocles, waiting for it to slash through their successes and achievements. For some it fuels an imposter complex: "One of these days I'm going to receive true justice." And the collector will no doubt demand compound interest. Yet for some there is an exhilarating sense of freedom and the opportunity for new beginnings.

Perhaps it is not so much realizing we have survived a divorce that is important as it is knowing that we have the hint of a hero in us. Hugo noted, "Life, misfortune, isolation, abandonment, and poverty, are battlefields which have their heroes; obscure heroes, sometimes greater than the illustrious heroes."

Could your divorce have been easier? Or was there something in this trauma that released some deep reserve within you? Did you discover some capacity that you had never before sampled? What was it in me that released my desire to lose and not regain almost 100 pounds? What motivated a Judy Cummings, a single parent, to hang in there, semester after semester at Purdue, until she achieved her academic triumph?

There are those who get good—even great—cash settlements from their divorce who still "whine." Others dash into seemingly successful second marriages to avoid the opportunity to do battle with themselves. They may live with doubt and boredom as a consequence. They possess no earned souvenirs.

Maybe that is why my VW is so important to me. It was about all I salvaged from the "Big D." I do not have to drive it. I could afford something better. But I've kept it for 130,000 miles as a trophy of sorts—a reminder of the adaptability of the human spirit.

I've made it. I want you to make it too.

I did not purposely choose to prove the self-prophecies wrong. I chose to survive. You may not "make it" in a year or even a decade. But you *will* make it if you *choose* to make it!

28   *Fear of Being Poor*

One of the first places a person feels a divorce is in the pocketbook. Lenore J. Weitzman, a sociologist at Stanford, discovered that women's living standards declined an average of 73% in the first year of a divorce, while men's *increased* 42%.[15] Although there is a ruckus over alimony (or child support or maintenance), the debate is academic. Most of it goes uncollected.

Margaret Heckler, secretary of Health and Human Services, reported that about 8.4 million women are raising children alone. Four million have been awarded child support. Look at the statistics:

47% collect child support

25% receive partial payments

28% receive nothing

In fiscal 1982, women and children were cheated out of $4 billion in uncollected child support.[16]

Financial planner Larry Burkett observed:

Estimated average income for a family of three	$22,000
Minimum *need level* for above	$16,000
Official *poverty level* for above	$13,000
Typical divorcée's income	$11,000

Burkett notes that the common single parent's "lifestyle is one of surviving from check to check, hoping that nothing breaks down, because there's no money to fix it."[17] Look at the breakdown of a typical single parent's income:

30% of net take-home pay goes to child care

40% of net take-home pay goes for rent

30% of net has to cover food, clothing, transportation, medical-dental care, etc.

That "etc." is a big category in a divorced person's budget.

Nicki Scott interviewed one divorced woman working at night in a doughnut shop. The woman interrupted the interview to warn her son,

> You eat your doughnut and drink your milk and play with your cars and don't scratch that table or make any noise or I'll take you out and blister your behind!
>
> "I keep him with me when I can," she said, wiping the table and refilling my coffee cup. "I can't leave him alone—he's a real terror. And I can't pay a sitter $2 an hour to watch him. I only clear about $125 a week. So I bring him here and hope he behaves."[18]

Part of the problem is that many couples look at a second job as a luxury. One woman reflected on her situation:

"I never thought of this job as my only income. I liked it, so I never looked for another one. I never had a career planned. I never thought ahead five years—or one year," she said bitterly.

"I didn't set goals or buck for promotions. I didn't work late every night to get ahead. I was content in my nice, safe little world. But now I'm 49 years old and I don't know what I'm going to do." [19]

". . . and they all lived happily ever after" is an American myth. Today there are an estimated five million childless older Americans, and this number is growing due to increased life expectancy. Many couples have looked forward to "growing old together."

Yet as one woman discovered,

I had a vision of our sunset years. After retirement, Jim and I would settle up north in our country home. It'd be something like 'On Golden Pond'—our golden years on a golden pond. But Jim had another plan. Now he's up north with her, and I'm down here with me. [20]

About 100,000 people over the age of 55 get divorced each year. Three factors will stimulate an increase in this number: an increase in the percentage of older people, liberalized divorce laws, and the loss of stigma.

When my daughter divorced, she was heartbroken, to be sure. But it was not the end of the world for her. She still has her children, a good job and a ton of divorced friends who 'celebrated' the end of her marriage. When I was left at 64, the children were grown and scattered. I had no job, less than no confidence, and I did not know one woman my age who was similarly dumped. [21]

A 62-year-old named Tanya pointed out that younger women can bounce back. "For me, it was a shameful, humiliating event that will leave me tarnished for the rest of my days." [22]

Barbara Cain, who interviewed several such senior divorcées at the Turner Geriatric Clinic at the University of Michigan, commented, "These women grope for answers in a psychic darkness." No one understands grandma's divorce.

However, the financial consequences are even worse. Many of these women have not worked outside their homes. Most will be eliminated from their husbands' pensions and medical insurance at an age when they cannot afford to be vulnerable.

If a man retires at age 70, his ex is entitled to half his benefit (but that amounts to only one-third of the total sum shared as a couple).

Those over 60 find it most difficult for anyone to understand. Barbara Cain concluded, "It is not only a loss but an insult. I gave him the best years of my life and look how he thanks me . . . ."

Many single-agains are turning a profound financial humiliation into a personal triumph.

Yes, financial survival is difficult. You may have to tighten your belt. But the chaos is only temporary. Brighter financial "tomorrows" are generally the products of financial baby steps.

You want to be valued for who you are—not for what you own. There are thousands who had their "season" of poverty, some of whom were even reduced to welfare, but who *chose* to chase away the fear and to say, "Poverty isn't permanent!" You can join that group or you can give up and let the welfare system and welfare philosophy tarnish your dreams.

29   *Fear of Being Alone*

"The fear of being alone," says the New York psychologist Miriam Greenspan, "heads the list of female terrors."[23] Having worked with many divorced men, I don't believe that females have an exclusive franchise on that fear.

It goes back to that early passage in Genesis, "It is not good for the man to be alone" (2:18). How many times have we heard that quoted? It doesn't take long in a separation until we realize we are vulnerable to all those "things that go bump in the night," and that there is no one to send to investigate.

Louise Bernikow calls it *solophobia*—the fear of being alone. Not just for a day, but forever. It reaches the outrageous level when a single person snarls, "Who would ever want to marry (or remarry) me?" Moreover, this particular fear has stages and degrees. Some newly-divorced people pass through it like a common cold; then there are seasons of especially great fear, like when the "Night Stalker" killer terrorized Los Angeles.

I once wrote an article called, "Does Loneliness Take Up All Your Time Alone?" in which I contended that loneliness and being alone are not synonyms. Not everyone agreed.

Many singles are armed with emotional night-lights. We do not want to be alone at work, in worship, at seminars, in bars, for a snack, in old age, or in our sleep.

Because of fear of being alone, some are desperate to form transitional relationships—someone to cruise K-Marts with on dateless Friday nights. One woman said, "I've paid a terrible price for this fear, cramming my calendar with things I didn't really care to do and people I didn't want to be with in order to avoid being alone."[24]

Take an inventory. Are there:

• movies you haven't seen because you don't want to go alone?

- restaurants you have avoided because you don't like being asked, "Party of one?" (No wonder the drive-in windows and frozen TV dinner sales have increased.)
- art exhibits or ball games you have missed because you didn't want to buy a solo admission?

Hey, old memories can't be totally forgotten. But by focusing on them you're missing out on new memories that you will cherish tomorrow.

Moments of aloneness are necessary to block out the din and roar of our noise-cluttered world. Do you use stereos, tape decks, televisons, or radios as "emotional baby-sitters"?

You may feel more alone at particular times—bedtime or mealtime. So throw a party for one. Have a predinner parade.

I look at aloneness as an investment—a time to recharge my emotional and spiritual batteries. Aloneness is a time to plant seeds. Besides, that way I can stand in front of a particular picture in a museum or gallery as long as I want to (it's amazing what you see that way). Ironically, *loneliness* can be a fog to block us from the harbor of *aloneness,* where time alone could provide the insight for the solution to a problem or crisis.

You need time to reflect, to meditate, to hear your own heartbeat, to test your own ideas. Some priorities must first be tested in the quiet of the spirit. It is not in the clamor that the best decisions are made.

One single reader laughs that she doesn't have time to be alone—with three small children. Her few moments of treasured aloneness are after the children are in bed.

In *Warm Reflections* I wrote:

I am alone. I have not cursed my aloneness
   nor have I welcomed it for a prolonged visit.

At this point I choose to be hospitable
   rather than face a duel.
Aloneness is an abstraction, a coloring book word,
   and the color I grant it decides whether I become
   the prisoner or the warden.

That, my friend, is a big choice, and one that only you can make!

30   *Fear of Holidays*

Holidays are family times. Just listen to the commercials, notice the ads. But for some, Christmas or any holiday can be a quiet season, a quiet day. It's not because they don't know the Christ of Christmas. Instead, someone with whom they have created Christmas memories is absent: through death, divorce, or separation. How many times have we said, "It won't be the same without you. . . ."

For many, there is one less present to buy, hide, and wrap; but also one less present to receive, one less surprise.

Take John, "celebrating" his first Christmas alone. His family had gone out of its way not to mention the hurt. However, Beth's absence was conspicuous. "Someone say something" seemed to be on every family member's tongue as they gathered on Christmas Eve. They figuratively tiptoed around John's assumed fear that someone might mention her name.

Finally, a niece, too young to understand the game, spilled the beans. "Where's Aunt Beth?" she asked. The question ricocheted through their hearts. Swiftly grandmother whisked her away for a convenient cookie.

Suicide rates go up after the holidays because people finally can no longer pretend their disappointments and hurts aren't there.

So here are some suggestions.

If you adopt a "Whatever you do, don't mention his (or her) name" rule, you'll make conversation strained and unnatural.

Consider some new times or locations. Maybe this is the year to celebrate on Christmas Eve rather than on Christmas morning. Perhaps a meal in a restaurant or another family member's home would be better than the traditional time and location.

If you keep old traditions, give those who are grieving an opportunity to say no or limit their involvement. Don't wait until the day before Christmas or the event to ask their intentions. But make sure you tell them that you still want them to participate. The wounded, in fact, may feel alienated while everyone is having such a good time. Like David's wife Michal, they watch "from a window" or at an emotional distance (2 Sam. 6:16). Some will feel guilty that they are putting brakes or dampers on everybody's festivity. Others may wish to withdraw into a cocoon and await the New Year.

Don't insist that old traditions be completed. If traditions produce a flood of discomfort or stress, they are counterproductive. Give a grieving or divorced person a way (even at the last moment) to take a "time out" or say, "I'll pass."

Be cautious about dismissing someone's feelings, and don't manipulate them into celebrating. Avoid statements like, "If you're not here, it just won't be the same!" or "I won't hear of you spending Christmas alone!" People can still be alone even when they are in the middle of a party.

Don't try to make it up economically. Gift giving as an anesthetic will only create more depression when the bills from the charge cards come due and stimulate February's depression.

Sometimes, through tears, we must say a sad good-bye to traditions just as we have to the people with whom we have shared those traditions.

The carol "I Heard the Bells on Christmas Day" is especially for the depressed during this season:

And in despair, I bowed my head.
"There is no peace on earth!" I said.
For hate is strong, and mocks the song,
Of peace on earth, goodwill to men!

Yet pealed the bells more loud and deep:
"God is not dead, nor doth He sleep;
The wrong shall fail, the right prevail
With peace on earth, goodwill to men!"

In his carol sung unfortunately only at Christmas, Isaac Watts suggested, "He comes to make his blessings known: far as the curse is found. . . ." Watts must have understood the Christmas blues, for three times he repeated the phrase, "far as the curse is found."

In the midst of your divorce, your curse, your wounding, Jesus comes to make his blessings known. Don't boycott the celebration. Give the season a chance. Reach out to others.

Part Five

PRIORITIES FOR LIVING

---

31 Recognizing Your Vulnerability

Your divorce will be a severe test of your spirit. Your first choice will be to (1) struggle to embrace the experience, or (2) somehow to avoid it.

Richard Gerber has identified four types of divorced persons:

- accusers—"It's all *your* fault!"
- avoiders—"Live and let live!" This person denies any responsibility for decision making and refuses to feel any pain.
- martyrs—"If only I could die!" This person enjoys describing the pain.
- resigners—"No use crying over spilled milk!" This person makes a premature surrender to the pain.[1]

Those who fall into one of these four traps do not grapple with their real issues. More than 2000 years ago, the prophet Jeremiah told the Jewish exiles to seek the peace and prosperity of the city to which God had carried them captive (Jer. 29:7). In other words, they were to embrace the experience of exile.

Ah, but we're Americans, who devour painkillers by the boxcar load. Our dentists anesthesize. We will do almost anything to avoid the unpleasant, the uncomfortable. Yet pain and suffering are a natural part of life.

I would add another category to Richard Gerber's list: the *triumpher*. While such individuals would prefer to pass up the experience, they sense an opportunity. They realize there are no easy answers, no 1, 2, 3 solutions. They also realize that their opponents are not their ex-spouses, but themselves.

A triumpher expects U-turns and detours. The road to triumph may resemble a roller coaster, with highs and lows, dips and thrills. The triumpher hangs on.

Although Gerber did not have such a category, he did describe such a person. A triumpher

- will feel the tragic consequences of this experience;
- will accept appropriate responsibility for the breakup;
- will integrate the scars of the loss with a new sense of hope that enables him or her to carry on when others would quit.[2]

Moreover, a triumpher discovers that this experience translates into other areas of life.

One verse of the book of Job has made a particular impression on me: ". . . the Lord made him prosperous again and gave him twice as much as he had before" (Job 42:10). That has been true of many divorced people as well—people who have chosen to embrace the painful struggle. Here are the key dynamics:

- admit your ambiguities and anxieties;
- recognize that you have power and freedom to make choices;
- accept responsibility for your choices;
- experience the pain of weakness and mistakes (don't blame others);
- trust the process;
- find hope in the possibilities for your future.

Mary's husband always kept both cars running. Now the slightest "bump-thump" sends her anxiety level off the scale. Worse, at a group meeting she learned about unscrupulous garage mechanics preying on recent divorcées. She was driving on the interstate in rush hour traffic when the car quit. She explained, "Luckily I got it over to the shoulder, and I just beat the steering wheel with my fist. 'It's all John's fault!' I screamed over and over. 'This old junker!' (He took the new car.)

"Then my seven-year-old calmly said, 'Mom, it's the gas, not the car.' We were out of gas!

" 'That's impossible!' I said. Sure enough, the needle was on *E*. So we hiked back to a filling station. To this day we laugh about the day *we* ran out of gas. I was so quick to blame the mistake on my children's father."

Triumphers rarely scream, shout, or snarl, "This is the last straw!" If they do, they quickly clarify it to "*nearly* the last straw." You can learn valuable lessons from such experiences.

Recognize your vulnerability.

There is one thing you can never steal from a triumpher: the belief in tomorrow.

---

32   *Reestablishing Your Identity*

Do you remember the story of the pigs who went to the market?

This little piggy went to market
and this little piggy stayed home.
This little piggy had roast beef
and this little piggy had none.
And this little piggy went "wee-wee-wee" all the way home.

"We/we" language is tough to break. You've been part of a duo for a long time. Some people can only think in pairs—it's been that way ever since they unloaded the ark. I remember the public outcry when Luci and Desi Arnaz broke up. People wondered if they could make it separately. Could they survive professionally as singles?

The problem is made more difficult by the number of years invested in a relationship, although if a marriage has been dying or dead for a long time, the grief may be significantly reduced. In situations like that, your you-ness can be more easily established. A lot of people are already emotionally divorced—they just haven't been to the courthouse yet.

Routines make it difficult. You know so much about your spouse (or thought you did!). A hundred little things may initially bring you pain. Your mate knew your favorite flavor of ice cream, favorite color, favorite perfume, birthdate, etc.

Now you have to abandon the we/we language. You've already had it happen. You're into a story and find yourself saying, "We . . . ."

Now you have to get used to saying:

- "*I* want. . ."

- "*I* prefer. . ."
- "*I'd* like to. . . ."

I found that one of the best ways to break the we/we language was to stop and say, "Excuse me, I meant to say," or, "I should have said. . . ." The first few times you may feel awkward or even foolish, but this is the best way to convince your subconscious that you're serious. This is happening!

You can survive anything you choose to survive.

Hear me out. Your ex may have done a "You!" number on you. But don't let that stop you.

Look at the example of Ramona Banuelos. Her husband brought her and four children into Texas and then said, "Adios!" She was in a desperate situation, and an illegal alien, too. *"No hablo inglés."*

But guess what?

She *decided* to survive her husband's betrayal. She chose not to go back to Mexico, back to poverty.

So she began making tacos (capitalizing on what she knew best). Ramona saved 10 cents out of every dollar she made. Eventually she went to a banker and borrowed money to start her own business.

As I'm writing this I am chuckling a bit over a story in this morning's paper. A woman is having her name removed from consideration for a federal judgeship. According to the article, she's afraid that as a single parent she couldn't live on the $72,000 a year salary.

Ramona's tacos were superb. Her survival instinct had given her confidence. She moved on. Eventually she ended up at the U.S. Treasury. She wasn't making tacos in the cafeteria, she was treasurer of the United States!

Now *that's* survival.

I'm not sure how bleak your situation looks. How could your situation be worse than Ramona's? At least you know the language.

But could your destiny—your goal—be any less?

You can choose to survive!

Remember, it's not so much what happens to you, but how you choose to respond.

Say that 10 times before you turn the page.

33   *Reexamining Your Priorities*

I can give myself time.

How will you know that you are really over the "Big D"?

- when you talk about your future more than your past;
- when you abandon your compulsion to marry again;
- when you decide to be over it.

I remember that first weekend, separated. "Whipped" is a better description. I had driven to Columbus, Georgia, to spend a few days with a college friend. After a light supper, we talked about the problem (up to that time we had talked about everything *but* the separation). David listened, occasionally asking questions. Then he dropped the bomb!

"You know it's going to take about four years to get over this, don't you?'' I felt like I had been kicked in the stomach. I snarled at him, "Four years? I drove four hours to hear this? I need comfort. . . . I don't think I can survive four weeks, let alone four years!" Some counselor!

"Well, I'm just telling you what I've discovered. . . ."

I repeated his words. *Four years.*

My wife had called me while I was on a road trip. I was staying in a Howard Johnson's (with all those light switches by the bed). With one swoop of my hand I turned everything off. I stumbled toward the window and slowly slid down on the floor. "I can't deal with this tonight. . . ." I thought, *Lord, help me make it to morning.* Then I sniffed the warm spring air, crawled across the room and into the bed, and fell asleep.

That was my first victory. A small one.

My divorce cost me a lot—an ordination and a missionary career. Suddenly, everything I had believed in was up for grabs. Nothing was certain. The wake of Jane's decision landed high on the shore of every one of my dreams.

David's good advice was to make no immediate decisions. Other friends, assuming I would do something rash, urged me to "be calm" or "give her time." They assumed she would return. Well, the advice was good, although the assumption was inaccurate. When she moved out she knew she wouldn't be coming back.

First I believed that she would be back by fall, then by January. Twice I thought she had changed her mind. So I waited. We had planned to vacation in Florida with my parents.

"Well, it's off," my mother said, and the disappointment was evident in her voice. In a split second I said, "No way. We're going!" I'm glad I made that commitment. Two weeks later, when I had a better understanding of my financial chaos, I would have cancelled.

Maybe you've faced such a decision. Do I keep a commitment or bail out? If the latter, is there a tactful way? There was no way

I could say to my parents, "I'm broke." I scraped up some money and massaged the credit cards.

Keeping that first priority changed my life. On that Florida trip I sat on the beach, on the decks, and on patios and drained my grief into three spiral notebooks that became my first book, *Warm Reflections*. If I had cancelled that trip, would I have written?

The next priority was counseling. Fortunately, I found a counselor with good credentials in a nearby city. Although it meant driving 30 miles one way and crying all the way home, it was worth it—the best money I have ever invested.

What I saw was a shambles, but the counselor stirred the ashes and found potential. "Someday," he predicted, "you'll help others." My initial response was, "Pass me the Kleenex."

You have to proceed with some things and delay others. My divorce sabotaged my plan to be a parent as well as to complete my doctorate at Vanderbilt.

But on May 10, 1985, almost a decade later, I received my Doctor of Ministry degree. That priority—so long delayed—became a reality.

And what about remarriage? Well, I assumed that I would remarry, that I would just cross out Jane and insert a new name in my memories. In time, surely, I would discover someone to make me forget that there had ever been a Jane. I assumed that remarriage would be the proof of my healing, the proof that I had "gotten over" my divorce.

Have I been surprised on that one! It's true that 85% of men marry within 14 months of their divorce. But the tenth anniversary of my D-Day has passed and my ring finger is still naked.

I learned that I needed time to heal, time to stub my toes. From that perspective, remarriage (particularly a "rebounder") would have been the worst thing that could have happened to me!

I'm not ruling marriage out completely. But if remarriage happens, it will be a pleasant surprise. If it does not happen, it will not be a bitter disappointment. My hope is that you, too, will come to embrace that philosophy on priorities.

One other priority was to get out of debt. The plastic spree was over. I remember my panic after I had cut up the cards. But to tell the truth, I waited too long. The cards were a type of amphetamine. Anytime I was down, I'd head for the nearest mall and buy something. "Poor me."

Wean yourself. Go through the withdrawals. The quicker you get to zero debt (and stay there), the easier your other priorities will be. Debt sabotages potential.

I couldn't write if I were up to my elbows in debt. Worrying about how I was going to pay the Visa bill would sap all my creativity.

Finally, I lost weight—over 100 pounds. Jane had always said she loved me "as I was" (46″ waist; 52″ shoulders), but since she had walked out, how could anyone else love me?

Single life and a desire to reassemble my shattered self-esteem helped me say yes to an exercise program designed by a great coach, Norm Witek.

Survival paved the way to "thrival." And in the process, I discovered a lot about me. I found I wasn't suited to be a minister or a missionary.

In the process, I discovered that "success" is a journey, not a line on a resume.

In the process, I learned that God sends people into our lives—sometimes to be Roto-rooters, unclogging our emotions. But God also sends remarkable people who help us find—even in the rubble—the first scent of tomorrow.

In the process, I have learned that the tragedies of life can be fertilizer for tomorrow's dreams.

So give yourself time. Go with the flow. Don't run away or yell "uncle" too soon.

Reexamine your priorities. Exclude any that do not clearly have your initials on them. Then go for it!

34   *Restating Your Values*

I can trust myself!

For the most part, Americans have destigmatized divorce. But for a very long time anyone who chose to divorce, especially on grounds other than adultery or desertion, was labeled. One woman said, "They might as well have branded a big *'D'* on my forehead. I could see it in their eyes."

Polly Baker of the Connecticut colony was divorced and then whipped, yet she dared speak in her own defense:

> I cannot conceive my offense to be of so unpardonable a nature as the law considers it. . . . I readily consented to the only offer of marriage that was ever made me. I have deluded no young man, nor seduced away any woman's husband. . . . You have already excluded me from the communion! You believe I have offended heaven and shall suffer everlastingly! Why then increase my misery by additional fines and whippings?[3]

In another case, in 1707, a woman at Plymouth received 30 stripes on her naked back and was thereafter required to wear the *A*. So much for redemptive compassion.

No wonder divorces were avoided; no wonder the divorced became social lepers.

Divorced people were thought to be loose, on the make. Admittedly, some were forced into survival economics. That reality made Jeannie C. Riley's "Harper Valley P.T.A." a number one hit in the country music charts.

When you divorce, some people conclude that you've changed, or that you had them fooled for a long time. This may be true even if you are a victim or recipient of an unwanted divorce.

But this is a time for restating your values, for clearing the air. Maybe you've already encountered a "friend" or business associate with overactive hormones. Or maybe you've already said a yes or no that you wish you could recall.

Every divorced person faces decisions. Some of these force us to admit our humanity. It's part of the process of growing.

I believe that you can trust yourself. You want good things. You want healing. Charlie Shedd once prayed, "Lord, help us to live so that we may always like what we see in the mirror."[4]

Some people cannot easily handle the freedom. But you can, because you can restate your values. It's the old Jewish confession, "But as for me and my household, we will serve the Lord" (Josh. 24:15).

Ethics and decency are not up for vote. You'll see statistics in *Cosmopolitan* that say 89% of divorcées are not celibate. Big deal. What is *your* decision? Are you going to play sexual "follow-the-leader"? Aren't you capable of making your own decisions?

Besides, there is a lot of science fiction in Singleland. People who claim to be living it up may be home with the shades drawn, watching reruns, and burping their Tupperware.

Alan Jones asked three great questions:

1. *Do I really believe that my life comes to me as a gift and that there is in me a terrific thing?* Historically the Christian faith has maintained that our bodies are the temple of the Holy Spirit and are to be honored. That means more than just "no extramarital sex." It means avoiding stress, overwork, poor diets. Yes, there is a terrific thing in you!

2. *Am I, in the middle of my own struggles, daring enough to ask for help, seek guidance, cultivate friendships?*

3. *Am I sincere in wanting to respond to my longings for growth, especially when I know and fear the revolutionary changes that may be involved?*[5] That's the part that we fear. Too many try to "fence in" their divorce: "I will only be affected in

these areas." Others have willingly embraced the experience—failures, triumphs, and uncertainties.

Can I redefine my faith in the midst of my hurt? Can I affirm that goodness will come? Yes. Values can make a big difference in how well you survive and thrive.

35   *Relinquishing False Innocence*

I can accept responsibility.

Society has a clever way of promoting divorce on the one hand and then condemning those who divorce. For example, we idolize romance: "He looked into her silky, shining eyes and he knew. . . that their love was meant to be." That's mild by today's standards. Three years, two babies, and 25 pounds later he wonders what he ever saw in her. She asks the same question about him.

Infatuation.

People get married because they had the equivalent of a hormonal thunderstorm, or they had sex and felt guilty, or she missed two menstrual periods, or they had bad home environments, or _____ (fill in the blank.)

In his book *Sex, Love, or Infatuation*, Ray Short says that the beautiful becomes boring. "Her Mr. Grand may turn out to be Mr. Bland, and his Miss Lovely has a good chance of becoming Mrs. Lousy." Short, who is a professor of marriage and family living, observed, "The wonder is not that so many of our marriages fail, but that so many manage somehow to survive."[6]

For too many, divorce is all but inevitable. The first step toward a divorce court is down the center aisle of a church. Short contends that "romantic love" or infatuation will hold "a marriage intact for no more than three to five years, even with a red-hot sex relationship thrown in."[7] Reality will eventually burst that bubble when the two who stared deeply into each other's eyes during dating now snarl and use their eyes as lances. The typical divorce process is, "You made me suffer and now you're going to pay for it!" Many divorce lawyers go for big settlements. Because of the way the legal system tears at the wounds, some of them never heal.

Christians have debated the question of divorce for 2000 years. We're divided into several camps:

- divorce on any grounds;
- divorce on the grounds of adultery;
- divorce on the grounds of adultery and desertion;
- no divorce.

People want to argue about the issue, even lacerate each other about it. I have conducted divorce seminars in every spectrum of the Christian community. I've been called "liberal" by some groups and "conservative" by others. I was handed one note that said, "You're no Christian! You're leading these people astray. This is a Christian conference and you don't belong here."

People take the theology of divorce seriously—in my opinion, too seriously. They let the question of whether divorce is a sin or not get in the way of ministering to the needs of those going through the experience. This kind of self-righteousness is something Jesus would not have tolerated.

I suspect that you have encountered some of this self-righteousness too. It leaves welts.

As a result, we find ourselves declaring our innocence and proclaiming our ex's guilt. This instinctive response comes from our childhood. "It was all his (or her) fault!" If pressed, we *might* concede, "Well all I did was. . . ."

My dad was tough. He didn't want to know what Jane did. He focused on *my* choices and *my* reactions.

As a counselor I've learned that there are at least two sides to every story. I've learned to gather as much data as possible before I form an opinion.

In my own divorce, I know when my healing began. I was locked into my feeling of innocence—"It was all Jane's fault." I played the role of helpless martyr. I had my lines down pat. I think I was convincing. But something was wrong.

I learned that I had to accept my fair percentage of the blame. I had to cash in my claim checks. I was a lousy husband: rude, inconsiderate, arrogant. I didn't listen carefully or to the end of the sentence.

Yet, as I faced that, I found healing.

But I didn't accept any more than my fair share.

Consider what happens if you don't own up to your own mistakes. You end up a casualty, a victim. You can end up blaming not only your ex but *all* men or *all* women.

Relinquishing our innocence is a gradual process. Initially, we're too splattered, too hurt. But as we heal, moments come for us to admit our errors, to admit we underestimated our own faults. I was moved by the prayer of confession used in Metropolitan United Church in Toronto on July 11, 1982:

O God, we confess
   our failure to be true
   even to our own accepted standards
   our choosing of the worse
   when we know the better;
   our unwillingness to apply to ourselves
      the standards of conduct
      we demand of others;
   our complacence toward wrongs that

do not touch our case
our oversensitiveness to those that do;
our slowness to see the good in our fellowman
    and to see the bad in ourselves;
our hardness of heart toward all our neighbor's faults
    and our readiness to make allowance for our own.
O Lord, forgive.

One counselee refused to accept even one percent of the blame. Now, as his third marriage ends, he faces a crossroads. It's decision time. If he had dealt with his responsibility and set aside his innocence, would he have had three ex-wives, all of whom were named "plaintiff"?

This *could* require you to ask your ex's forgiveness. You may tell me, "You've got to be joking!" But I'm serious. Yet it does take guts and courage. I know from personal experience how difficult it is.

"OK," you may grudgingly agree, but only if your ex goes first!

Sorry—it doesn't work that way.

Gerald Jampolsky's marvelous book, *Love Is Letting Go of Fear*, includes a great cartoon. Over a man's eyebrows is a theatre marquee with the words: "Old Films. Now Playing Inside."[8]

I believe Richard Nixon could have stayed in office *if* he had owned up to his choices and asked the forgiveness of the American people. Smart people don't want to harbor grudges.

Ten simple words could open up the future for you:
- "I am sorry. . . ."
- "I was wrong. . . ."
- "Will you forgive me?"

You don't have to air all the dirty linen or do a blow-by-blow description. A simple, "I wasn't perfect" is a great starter.

You can accept responsibility.

Author Judith Krantz observed, "When I look at friends who have divorced, I see that with their second or third husbands they finally made the compromise (and decisions) which would have kept them married to their first husbands if they had figured it out then."[9]

Do yourself a favor: cash in your innocence. Accept your fair share of the responsibility.

36   *Reducing Your Manipulability*

I can make good decisions.

Divorce is a big decision. Hopefully it was one of the most serious, thoughtfully considered decisions that you have ever made. What will this experience mean?

Boxing is a brutal sport, yet some of its terminology may be helpful for this discussion.

Many matches are 15 rounders. If the fight "goes the distance" it will be up to the scoring system to decide the winner. During the early rounds, managers in both corners will be calling out, "Watch that right!" After three minutes the fighters are back in the corner for a breather.

There are matches that are mismatched from the first round. Others fall apart midway. Then a referee steps in and stops the fight; one boxer is taking too much punishment. That's called a TKO—a technical knockout. There are fighters who will plead, "Let me fight." That means, "Let me get my brains knocked out."

How many marital boxers have held on too many rounds? After having been bloodied, they stagger back to a corner to get ready for the next round. I wonder if we don't need people who can stop the fight.

Perhaps you have learned that you cannot always trust the people who profess to be "in your corner." They may know all the maneuvers and techniques, but you are the one getting beat up on. How many boxers have been injured because of a manager's pride? There's always the hunch that "the next round is mine."

OK, so you made (or inherited) a decision to divorce. Guess what? There are people who will now try to pull your strings, and you'll end up feeling like a puppet:

- *your ex.* A divorce doesn't eliminate an ex; it only changes the relationship and the stakes. Some exes are easy to get along with. Others are master manipulators.

- *your children.* Initially there will be a vacuum. Your children may try to mount a coup, or at least test their limits. They may try to pit you against your ex. They know how to read you and how to hit below the belt.

- *your parents.* Some parents want to declare "marital law." Some stand in the way of reconciliation. Some have their "I told you sos" all lined-up and ready to be played. Some parents are "stringers." They offer gifts . . . but with a string, a catch.

- *holidays.* How you struggle with memories of "Christmas past"! It's even worse when old Santa has to tighten his belt. It's tempting to try to best your ex with a little "bribery" or one-upmanship. The kids will initially love your gifts. But gift giving to gain affection sometimes boomerangs.

- *horror stories.* Horror stories have led many people to assume the worst in their ex, based on the misbehaviors of a friend's ex. Take the horror stories in stride; remember, there are usually two sides to them.

● *your lawyer.* It is *your* divorce—not your attorney's. Remember, he or she works for you. Some have big reputations to defend. They may quickly determine that you don't have a lot of money. Or your ex's attorney may be a lawschool buddy, so you become a casualty to the "good ol' boy" network. At times you will hear, "I'm not telling you what to do. . . ," but wait for the "but."

● *religious authorities.* I learned of a woman who was married to a bisexual. On business trips he frequented gay baths and bars; as a result he gave her VD three times. Each time he repented and was forgiven. But the next VD infection was proof that he had not changed his behavior. As a result of believing her pastor, who told her she *could not* divorce him, she will die.

● *your finances.* Many decisions are made because of money. Has "we can't afford it" become common in your home? There may be occasions when you made a bad decision because you were frustrated by lack of money, especially if your ex was living "high on the hog." It's easy to sacrifice your future on the altar of the moment. Finances can frustrate, but they must not manipulate. Only if you stop charging will that credit card balance shrink.

Be an adult. Avoid even subtle manipulation. Expect it, but then respond to it. Resist. The more decisions you make, the more confident you will become. It's a lot like learning to drive a stick shift. That clutch can be a pain, but once it is mastered, you're in business.

Remember, you don't need a romantic rescuer, either. Some have great emergency room skills. You become their project. But they will expect compensation, and it may well be sexual. A premature romantic relationship will also short-circuit your learning to cope, and it could well sabotage your growth.

Be on guard.

37   *Rejecting the "You-Talk"*

"You know what your problem is?" Great cliché, especially when punctuated with a jabbing finger. And when you hear these words you suspect that the speaker is about to answer his or her own question.

"You-talk" is destructive, dangerous, and abusive. It's difficult to say in soft voices. Sometimes, in the heat of the moment, we say things that later we can't believe we said. Words, emotions, and attitudes race over our lips like a kayak over a falls.

Why is it that Americans feel so duty-bound to state their opinions? to say "If you ask me . . ." when generally no one asked them?

How about this one: "I'm going to give him a piece of my mind!" To which a friend quipped, "Are you sure you can afford that?"

At times we flee rather than fight. Silence seems a wise response. Proverbs says, "A gentle answer turns away wrath" (15:1). Waitley and Witt commented on that verse by saying,

> NEVER trample on the other person's ego. Sarcasm, insults, and intimidation have a negative boomerang effect. A conversation must end as a double-win; if the other person feels he has lost face, the [argument will intensify].[10]

We don't know how to sidestep opinions. We think we have to one-up the you-talker. We retort:

"Oh yeah. . . . ?"

"What would *you* know?"

"Says who?"

"Well, here's what I think of that!"

Some people resort to four-letter words or obscene gestures, none of which leads to better communication.

Waitley recommends:

Sidestep any attempt by the other person to belittle you. If the conversation heats up, stay calm. Diplomatically return the tone to the topic at hand. If necessary, call a time out. Arrange to meet on another day.[11]

That sounds cowardly. So we may say, "Let's get to the bottom of this!" One of my favorites is, "You started this, now I'm going to finish it!" Sometimes both the conversation and the friendship *do* end up finished.

No one can make you feel second class without your cooperation.

Unfortunately, some of us grew up in families where we did not feel affirmed. So we married with a deficiency in affirmation that we hoped a mate would fill. However, your self-esteem does not come from your mate or how well you fill any of the cultural roles or rules. Your self-worth comes from your Creator and from within. We have a Creator who calls us by *our* names (Isa. 43:1) rather than a collective "you," who dreams dreams for us, who hurts when we hurt.

Some marriages turn pathological because two people frantically attempt to shore up each other's sagging, fragile egos.

In fact, one top agenda of divorce should be to gain and improve your communication skills. Divorce—or the threat of divorce— is the stimulus by which some people become assertive.

Small support groups such as Divorce Recovery can help us learn to share, to open up. We discover that there are people who want to hear what we have to say, who listen all the way to the end of the sentence. What a liberating surprise!

You-talkers are like people who drive their cars on beaches without permission. They will leave their tire tracks across your soul. So be assertive—put up a few "No Trespassing" signs. Do not defend yourself by:

- out-talking or out-shouting them;
- beating them at their own game;
- going for their jugular.

You are special. Insist on your dignity.

38   Recognizing Dead-Ends

You've no doubt seen those signs with arrows going in all directions: 989 miles to Austin; 700 miles to Knoxville. Or perhaps you've had the experience of missing your turn in one of those interstate spaghetti interchanges. "Oh no!" you mumble as you sail pass the exit.

Many divorced people have felt the same way. There are so many advice givers. I have not forgotten the twice-divorced friend who suggested, "Go for her jugular! Nail her before she nails you." Ironically, the same guy later set aside our friendship momentarily while he dated my ex.

My dad always studied maps before he drove. And we generally stuck to the main roads—ignoring enticing side excursions. Well, divorce is a journey of sorts—of the emotions. While there are no specific maps to study, there is a main road to recovery. That journey makes you a different person. And generally it rewards those who stay between its white lines.

However, let's note some of those side roads.

1. Iron man/iron woman. "Hey I can take it!" they boast

stoically. So if they get wounded, they quickly rivet another layer of metal over the wound. Many tap their armor and smile, "I am divorced! I am invincible!"

2. Sleazing. "Swinging single on the loose" read the bumper sticker. Perhaps this divorcée had long ago become bored with monogamy and was now "making up for lost time." Or she may have been out to hurt someone, to get even. She may hold all men guilty for a husband's betrayal.

3. Anesthetizing. "It hurt too much." This person looks for a drug to dull the pain: sex, alcohol, cocaine, money, or any combination thereof.

4. Postponing. "I can't deal with this!" moans the classic postponer. In a few weeks or months, maybe. This is often the case with the highly-motivated person who merely works harder. Or as one single parent quipped, "I don't have time to deal with this. I have four mouths to feed."

5. Martyrdom. "I have the worst divorce in the world" exclaimed one woman. Divorced people eagerly exchange war stories with a "Can you beat that?" attitude. One would think that after years of working with thousands of divorced people I could say, "I've heard it all," but I haven't. There are always new twists. The martyr gets a psychological payoff from the experience of telling horror stories.

These are negative patterns. Let's look at some others.

6. Rebounding. "Least amount of time divorced, the better." I saw a book called *How To Get a Husband in Thirty Days*. I wonder if it was written by a divorced woman. A rapid remarriage or live-in relationship is the worst of the side roads.

Why?

• *Your focus is wrong.* Rebounders do not focus on what is best for them, but on a friendly or unfriendly competition with their ex. Some attempt to prove something to their ex: "See? Somebody loves me after all!"

• *Your timing is wrong.* You need time to heal. Ask yourself, "How long did I know my first mate?" Now, with all that time and it still didn't work out, how is this instant relationship going to survive? "Instant" romances often led to second divorces.

● *Your motive is wrong.* Marriage is to be a mutual benefit. When your pulse quickens and your heart beats frantically, what you have is infatuation, not love.

I wish I could impose a quarantine on the recently divorced. I'd like to place them in an environment in which they could heal. Some are so fragile and delicate. They are too precious to be bed bait.

Believe me, I know that it hurts to sleep alone—to be alone on those special, red-letter days. But my hunch is that the loneliest person in your zip code last night was a married adult rather than a single. Or possibly it was a person in a hasty second marriage muttering, "What a fool I am!"

Life rewards the plodders and strugglers. I'm not trying to delay anything. But consider this analogy. When I came home from school, my mom generally had snacks to tide me over until supper. The snacks varied from apples to brownies. Often I wanted more. But my mother would say, "We don't want to spoil your appetite. I have something that's good for you." Life is the same way. There's a feast of good days coming. But if you want to snack on empty calories of the moment, you'll spoil your appetite for the best.

There is value in staying on the main road to healing. Give your dreams a chance.

39　*Refurbishing Your Self-Image*

Key West, Florida, has been named "the Conch Republic" and "the last resort." Natives are called conch. People who first came to Key West built wood houses (a rarity in Florida). Naturally, in time, residents began building concrete block houses in Old Town—bespoiling the setting.

However, of late, Key Westers have really gotten into remodeling and refurbishing old houses, restoring them to their prime. Many of the efforts are astounding.

While jogging I saw something that really pleased me. A builder had built on the front of a concrete block house a wooden Conch-style addition. No longer will anyone see the concrete blocks.

I believe a similar process can happen with people, particularly with self-esteem. Divorce assaults a self-image like a hurricane overwhelms Florida shoreline.

You may be like me. Your self-esteem was deflated before you divorced. Now you've gone from deflated to something even worse.

I still remember my first encounter with one of those Bible totin', Bible quotin' folks who mangled me with selected proof texts: "God hates divorce!" he told me. From his tone, I suspected that he hated divorced people as well. Moreover, I was certain this fellow was following God's lead.

I also asked myself, "Who would want to marry me?" I could list several reasons why no one would. Besides, in our society it's difficult for someone to have a healthy self-esteem with a 46" waist (unless you're a Sumo wrestler).

I assume you know what you'd like to change about yourself. Ask yourself three questions.

- Can I do anything about it?
- If so, am I willing to pay the price?
- If not, am I willing to change my attitude?

Put this book down. I want you to give these three questions some serious thought.

Is a diet in order? I'm surprised someone hasn't developed "the divorced person's diet." I know that one's calorie intake is often significantly altered during or after a divorce. There are:

- those who don't have money to eat;
- those who have no appetite; and
- those who use food as a crutch.

Diets need to be realistic. When I weighed 285 pounds, my first goal was not to lose 100 pounds, but 10. I decided:

- Not to even buy junk food.
- Not to eat or snack in the bedroom.
- To befriend vegetables: carrots, celery, etc.

Don't eat when or because you're lonely, have no date, or the kids are with your ex. It's easy to inhale a few thousand calories to anesthetize the pain. If you resist the urge to snack the next time you snarl, "Who would want me?" there will be less guilt.

Befriend your bathroom mirror. Weigh yourself every day. Write the weight down on a sheet of paper attached to the mirror. Go for the best. Don't eat junk food. Watch the greasy foods (besides, it will be better for your digestion, since your tract may be upset with stress already).

Eliminate the term "fat slob" from your vocabulary. You may be overweight or even obese. But that does not make you a slob!

Let me recommend a book: *Diets Don't Work* by Charles Swartz (Breakthru Publishing, rev. ed. 1984). It helped me lose weight and enhanced my self-esteem.

Be kind to yourself. Marge's husband had left her for a "petite little thing" after 23 years of marriage. "And he told me he liked big women!'' she fumed. "OK, maybe I've grown a little here and there . . . but so has he."

It's interesting that weight does not seem to be as much of a factor in the social lives of men. Junior is "stout," not fat. But heaven help a woman if she is "five pounds over"!

So Madge sends out a "poor me" message. Men on the make catch the radar signals. More than once she has ended up in bed with them, anesthetized by, "Who said you were fat? You're just healthy!" Each time she hates herself more and binges more. It's a continuous cycle of defeat.

Maybe it's time for a commitment to developing positive self-esteem.

Poor self-images are pesky houseguests.
Maybe it's time you evict the little brats!
I'd like to do the eviction process for you.
But only you can throw them out!

Be good to yourself—evict them!

40   *Realigning Guilt and Responsibility*

I can let go!

On my kitchen wall hangs a plaque that reminds me of an important truth for survival: "Our faults are not as objectionable as the methods we think up to hide them!"

Dr. Frank Freed jolted me with a simple question: "What are *you* pretending not to know?"

How would you answer his question? What are *you* pretending not to know?

Two thousand years ago the apostle Paul said that we should speak "the truth in love" (Eph. 4:15). Truth is not always pleasant, but it is essential.

Some people perceive themselves as truth-spreaders. They are blunt and tactless. Maybe your ex fits that bill. But it's tempting to ignore some of the data about ourselves and our choices.

Marge, for example, frustrated me, because she didn't want to deal with guilt. She refused to admit the truth about her ex. On many occasions he had been abusive. I have little sympathy for mate-beaters. God didn't design anyone to be a doormat or a punching bag.

Finally, in frustration, I said, "Some people want to be beaten."

"Oh!" she howled. "I am offended that you would say such a thing." (It was high melodrama, to say the least.)

Finally, I laid Frank's great question on her. "Marge, what are you pretending not to know about your ex?"

She countered by saying that he had stopped the abuse, that he had not beaten his second wife.

"Marge, how do you know for sure? He may be just storing up his rage and anger, waiting to unleash it with a fury you missed."

Because of her religious background, Marge wants to be a martyr. C. S. Lewis described this motive in *A Grief Observed:*

> We want to prove to ourselves (and to others) that we are lovers
> on the grand scale, tragic heroes; not just ordinary privates in the
> huge army of the bereaved, slogging along and making the best
> of a bad job. [12]

Lack of realigning the guilt and responsibility keeps us tied to our past. I wrote in *Jason Loves Jane,*

> Oh, I've loved you dramatically
> and I've held on to you
> even after you asked me to let go.
> It is as if I am trying to prove to all our friends
> how much I loved you.
> There was a nagging fear that I thought
> that perhaps they thought that
> maybe I wasn't such a good husband, after all,
> "Why would she leave him?" [13]

Some people take more than their fair share of the guilt and blame; that was Jane's response after reading my first two books. Sometimes we reassume the blame after encountering people who are rabidly antidivorce, the ones who think divorce must be avoided at all costs.

Mary is 61 and the mother of two talented professionals. She had a brief marriage during World War II. Her family was scandalized. She bore the stigma until she met and married Bill.

Once, while on vacation, they heard a minister preach against remarriage, which he labeled "perpetual adultery." "Every time you have sex you're commiting adultery. Every time!" he exclaimed. First Mary's sex life died. Then, slowly, her marriage was strangled, although they stuck it out for the sake of the kids.

Only after her husband's death and her own prolonged counseling did she find a faint glimpse of hope—a taste of forgiveness. She moaned, "All those years I was already forgiven. That preacher was wrong. I believed him and destroyed my marriage!"

Take a good look at your guilt load. Is it past time for a reassessment? If you have confessed your sins to God, then you are forgiven. Why not forgive yourself, too?

41   Resisting the "Demons"

I can always change channels or tune out the negatives.

"Zapping" (the practice of switching channels to avoid commercials) has a lot of advertising agency executives worried. With the development of remote controls, people no longer *have* to watch commercials, particularly bad ones. Zap! Many TV fanatics love to zap. It gives them a sense of power over Madison Avenue.

Within your mind is a different kind of zapper your Creator thought you ought to have. All of us have pesky little "demons" that love to carry placards and chant out slogans:

- "You're no good!"
- "You're a slob!"
- "Who'd want you?"
- "Marital reject!"
- "What a loser!"

How many times have you overhead their impish little giggles punctuating the accusation? But for some reason you don't zap them. You actually listen to them. Each time they get a little bolder, a little more brazen.

Some are great actors. On the stage in your mind they recreate insults and indignities, often in living color.

Of course, you can yell "Scat!" until you're hoarse. I think a better alternative is positive overkill. Begin packing in new memories, positive ones. Give yourself a hand for the small victories and achievements, like fixing an appliance or standing up to that ogre garage mechanic who planned to overcharge you!

Replay that achievement. Put up on the marquee: "Now Playing: The Achievements of _____."

Run the achievement in slow motion. By packing in the positives, you effectively crowd out the negatives. You simply don't give them time on the program.

Or suppose you're lying in bed having a mini pity party, lightly caressing the empty half of the mattress. Reach for the "hit list" of things to do instead of a pity party. How about starting by cleaning that disgusting bathroom shower curtain? So what if it's 2:00 A.M.? If it's a good time for a pity party, it's a good time to tackle that shower curtain. The alternative will burn out the negative energy.

Finally, remember that there might be a kernel of truth in the "demon's" accusation. You may have strengthened its hand by ignoring some truth.

For example, I used to wake up at 4:00 A.M. Some of the videos that replayed in my mind were hard to handle. But when I learned to cut away the "bone and fat," I found the substance of the accusation and responded to that.

Generally the "demons" are cowards. If you are persistent, they will pack up and leave. But keep that zapper handy. And don't hesitate to use it!

42   *Resisting Bargain-Basement Life-Styles*

I can be good to myself!

All of us face options of "discount" life-styles.

Sex is the first to rear its ugly head. You want companionship instead of a wrestling match. Quickly you discover that the rules have changed. Intercourse is expected by the phrase (and a lift of the eyebrow), "Your place or mine?"

Many divorced women learn that divorced men do not take "No" seriously. One angry woman said, "I think their brains are between their legs! It's like they have just rediscovered puberty."

For others, sex is a game, an anesthesia.

Often because of acute loneliness people say yes to discount invitations. Then you wonder if he (or she) will call the next day or remember your name the next time you see them.

In our world it's easy to share the sheets but not the soul. Someone has said that this generation has shifted the fig leaf from the genitals to the heart. Divorce often results in strangers becoming bedfellows.

● *Live-ins and sleep-overs* are another discount life-style. Some do not feel guilty about the sex, but they resent having to hide it from their children. Sneaky sex. Naturally children become confused when there is a succession of mates in their single parent's bed. (In section 25, "Fear of Rejection," I deal with specific objections to living together or "auditioning.")

But remember, a live-in relationship closely resembles a marriage. As your mother used to say, "Play with matches and you'll get burned."

• *Sloppiness* is another variation. "Why should I bother to look nice? to take care of myself? Especially if I don't have a date? Besides, who wants to go out with a woman (or a man) 25 pounds overweight with three children? I concede that this can make dating difficult. But if you don't control yourself, those 25 pounds could become 35, 45, or even more.

For your own self-esteem, be neat! Be clean! And take care of your body! You don't know where or how you'll meet someone whom you would like to have notice you!

• *TV-itis* is even worse. Waitley reports that the *average* American spends 28 hours per week watching the tube.[14] It's easy to form a one-flesh relationship with a TV set. It becomes your comforter, your friend. You find yourself talking back to it. It comes on as soon as you walk in the door from work; it goes off after you are fast asleep.

Now cable TV will bring "R" or "X" rated sex right into your living room and stimulate your "poor me!" feelings. You may end up masturbating—and then feel awkward or guilty about that.

Besides, you need quiet time to think, to hear your own heartbeat, to get in touch with the gifts that are within you.

• *Boredom.* Are you in a rut? Life may be passing you by. Look at the "things to do" section in your newspaper—(you'd be surprised how many things are free or inexpensive). Shake up your life a little! Try something new!

• *Drinking and drugs.* It's tempting to drown your problems with a drug—whether alcohol, cocaine, sex, or food. But the problem is still going to be there.

Singles' bars are the dungeon of divorcedom. Men with smooth lines and fragile egos see you as an "opportunity."

No one wants to go home alone. But seldom are there any *real* conversations in bars. "Do you live around here?" (Someone actually asked that in a bar on a singles' cruise.) "Come here often?" "Don't I know you?" I realize that you may be desperate for adult conversation (especially if you are a single parent with small children). But a singles' bar is untalk. Babble.

(Now I am going to sound like your mother.) This life-style wreaks havoc on your finances; it costs money to barhop. And there is danger: someone who in the dark smoke looks like the Right One could be the Wrong One. The evening could end up with date-rape or worse. And he could give you something to remember him by (like Herpes). Forget the bars!

● *Mothering.* Some divorcées seem to want special projects. They adopt a loser or sponsor "the loser of the month." They do his laundry, clean, iron, mend—get him back on his feet, all in the hopes of reforming him. They hope he will be appreciative. Meanwhile, he takes it for granted and moves on to someone else when the opportunity arises.

How many divorced people are there who have run emergency rooms for emotionally wounded people?

I don't think most people deliberately choose discount life-styles and relationships. Somehow we get suckered into them. "Go with the flow" or "I don't care anymore!" are our rationalizations.

I may sound like I'm preaching at you. But I meet many people who have a second or third set of tire tracks across them.

Be good to yourself. Use "*no* power." Be loyal to your best interests. Go first class.

43   *Resuming Custody*

One thing is for sure—divorce gives you custody of yourself. You may not want it, but you've got it.

Perhaps you're in what I call "limbo chaos."

- You can't get your checkbook to balance.
- You can't keep your laundry clean.
- You can't make ends meet.

So you decide you need "someone." Actually, some men want a combination of a maid + mother + nurse + playmate ("Only those with experience need apply!"). Some women want a handyman + financier + disciplinarian + a little Tom Selleck for good measure.

Custody is tackling the tasks you least want. We're still gender-specific in this culture. Males tend to work on cars; women tend to clean and cook. But now you get to tackle it all yourself. Are you threatened by automobile mechanics and television repairmen? Are you at a loss when the washing machine sabotages your permapress?

Custody means *you* have to take charge.

"But I don't want to!" OK, but the situation isn't going to go away. Your washer is *not* going to wash your clothes by itself. Nor will your lawn mow itself.

You would be surprised to know what you can do! The wife of one of my friends left two days before Thanksgiving. The family had been used to the big T-day pig-out. "Well," he snapped, "I can do it myself!" It was like planning the invasion of Europe during World War II. Charts, graphs, etc.

At 7:00 A.M. he was up. The peas were ready by 7:25! The candied yams by 8:15! The salad by 8:30! The cranberries by 8:32! Unfortunately, the turkey wasn't ready until 6:30 P.M. By that time his kids had cleaned out the peanut butter and were threatening patricide.

That was the day he discovered that you don't just peel the wrapper off the turkey and stick it in the oven.

The next year the family council met two weeks before T-day. "Well, guys, what do you want for Thanksgiving?"

"Chili!"

"On Thanksgiving?"

"Dad, remember last year? Chili you can make." Years have passed and the boys are all grown and married. But they and their friends still come back for a bowl of Texas chili. They started a new family tradition on Thanksgiving.

Eliminate the phrase, "Oh, I might fail," from your vocabulary.

Custody offers you freedom and responsibility. You have the freedom to cook chili on T-day. For some, this will be your first real taste of freedom. If you don't want to change the sheets, don't. How many marriages are hamstrung by unadventurous mates who don't want to try the Irish-Chinese restaurant on the corner because they *might* be disappointed? They'd rather be bored at Burger Doodle.

But a word of caution is in order. Give yourself time to make up for lost time. Maybe you've been on an "emotional diet." When the Vietnam POWs returned, they didn't immediately feed them 16 ounce T-bones with all the trimmings. They gave them time before they "killed the fatted calf."

First-person singular custody can be scary. But it can also be delicious. It's a great start toward emotional healing and growth.

Don't waste your energy on minor-league dreams. Go for the gold! Take charge!

44   *Repairing the Damage*

I can be healed!

The statistics tell us very little about what's really going on among divorced people.

I remember my first fender-bender as a teenage driver. Fortunately those aren't capital offenses. I learned a great deal through the process. My father wouldn't go to the insurance office with me. He said that I had to assume some responsibility to deal with the damage.

Just as car wrecks have made "body shops" big business in this country, there should be a similar process with divorce. My colleagues Bill Flanagan and Jim Smoke helped launch a healing movement called Divorce Recovery. It was visionary and compassionate. I only wish there were Jims and Bills in every zip code.

I remember seeing a sign in California for the "Holy Ghost Repair Shop." I was instantly offended. But as I thought more about it, I grew kinder. The Holy Spirit is the great distributor of mercy and compassion in the world. The Spirit guides people to reach out and touch each other. The Spirit is called the *paraclete,* or the "one who comes alongside," or "the helper."

We need to understand the process of repair. Take a look at these steps:

1. Get reliable estimates. What will it cost in energy? Some will offer you cheap solutions for your wound. Some will suggest a hasty second marriage or a live-in arrangement as a quick fixer-upper.

2. Make a commitment. In the book of Genesis, Jacob wrestled with a man all night. He tightened his grasp when the man started to flee. The man pleaded, but Jacob growled, "I will not let you go unless you bless me" (Gen. 32:22-26). My counselor concluded one very traumatic session with that statement. Divorce is one of those experiences that either makes you better or bitter. It was my choice, he suggested. "Don't let go of it, Harold," he added, "until it blesses you."

I laughed. I was nearly broke and he was suggesting that I would find a blessing in all this. I questioned my wisdom in staying with this counselor.

But he was right!

In my settlement I got a VW, a color TV, and a washer and dryer. The basics for masculine survival. That VW is a trophy of sorts to me. It now has 130,000 miles on it and has provoked a lot of teasing. This past winter, I was in a fender-bender and received some cash to "repair" the car. I had to get estimates. One man annoyed me by saying, "Who would spend money to fix this?"

After my vacation I went to pick up the VW at the repair shop. I couldn't believe it. What a beauty! In the bright sunshine the blue metallic finish sparkles.

What did it take to repair the damage?

- someone wanting it done;
- someone believing the work could be done;
- many hours of sanding, filling, and priming.

Oh, I could have bought some of those spray paints at K-Mart and done the job, but it wouldn't have been first class. I had them repair it with the best materials.

I believe the damage of divorce can be repaired. I am stronger because of my divorce. I received an official reprimand from my denomination for saying that in an article in the *Nashville Banner,* but I still believe it. I paid the price; I invested in myself.

There is nothing that can happen to you that you cannot survive. It is going to take more than a divorce to keep you from pursuing a dream. Part of it is timing. For example, divorce kept Adlai

Stevenson out of the White House. But it didn't keep Ronald Reagan out a generation later. And some of the most conservative Christians in the country supported him.

3. *Give yourself time.* Forget about remarriage for the time being. Make a commitment to yourself—to explore all of your own potential before you explore the potential of another.

4. *Get involved in a divorce support group.* If you don't have one, start one. By helping others heal, you get great side benefits for your own healing. And the example you set in repairing the damage will help someone else.

45   *Recovering from Bad Decisions*

It happened. Somehow, in a weak moment or perhaps in anger, you made a dumb, *dumb!* decision.

There are dumb decisions.

Then there are *dumb! dumb!* decisions.

For Beth, a moment of acute loneliness led to a sexual encounter between the sheets. Actually, it was little more than mutual masturbation. Afterward, he was quiet and Beth was guilt-ridden. And for Beth, the experience led to more serious consequences.

Yet Beth learned some good lessons from a bad decision. A mistake can be disastrous and still be a great classroom to learn more about yourself and about others.

Beth cautions friends now going through divorce to give themselves time and room to heal.

Most likely you want another relationship. But you want it on the best possible terms. Believe me, you don't want a second divorce. And neither did the thousands who will go through their second or third divorce this year. Like you, most of them wanted little more than an emotional Fourth of July on a cold winter night. They wanted someone to want them again. And they wanted to lie close to someone, too.

You need time to heal. Be good to yourself. Don't let one mistake pave the way for a bigger one!

There are intimacy-bandits out there. Like the robbers who preyed on stagecoaches in the Old West, they are waiting to ambush you. They gain some satisfaction from one-night stands because they have a limited capacity for friendship or emotional warmth. They translate your pain to their advantage. And they get rather good at it. Confident. They boast about their latest conquests with buddies.

And they don't all hang out in singles bars. Some prefer church groups or singles groups. They find your initial no a challenge. A no adds to the thrill. There is an old saying, "Salesmanship doesn't begin until the customer says no."

Mistakes are survivable and educational. Here's how:

1. Know your needs. You're a healthy, normal, red-blooded, single adult. You have needs. Don't try to deny them.

2. Accept your responsibility. Maybe you were swept off your feet. *Maybe.* But it takes two to tango.

3. Find the lesson. So many people attempt to block mistakes out of their mind. But if that happens prematurely, you're unlikely to learn the lesson. Then you may make more mistakes, possibly with worse consequences. When Henry Ford bought Thomas Edison's labs, he also purchased the trash barrels. He wanted to learn from Edison's failures as well.

4. Forgive yourself. I suggest that you be kind with yourself. Also, a good counselor may help you make the pieces fit together better.

5. Join the crowd. Whatever your mistake, you're not the first one to have made it. It's a lot like a stubbed toe—it hurts for a little while, and then you get over it.

I'm not being flippant. I've met people who were so humiliated by their mistake and so anxious that no one know about it that they punished themselves for years over it.

A mistake can be a great classroom.

46 Redeeming the Experience

I can be an M.I.P. (miracle-in-progress).

VIPs get preferential treatment. They have status—clout—influence. People return their phone calls promptly. I am proposing a new category—MIP: miracle-in-progress!

Most of us never see miracles because we are skeptical and analytical. Some miracles are instantaneous. Others take weeks, months, years, even a lifetime.

We want instant entertainment, instant coffee, and instant relationships. What is worse, we want instant solutions. But a miracle needs time, energy, and risk.

I remember believing that a miracle would save my marriage and prevent a divorce. Jane would come back. It would be just like those old movies where the convict is strapped into the electric chair, and at the last possible moment, when the warden's hand is on the switch, the governor grants a stay of execution. Just in the nick of time! Down to the wire!

But you may not get your miracle. Then what?

You survive.

You get on with the program of being a miracle-in-progress.

I am now six feet tall. But once I was two feet, then thirty inches, then three feet. My parents, like many others, made those little growth notches on the wall. It's difficult to believe that I was ever that short, but there on the doorjamb is the proof (and the date).

Back then I couldn't believe that I would ever grow this tall. All I had was my parents' assurances that I would.

When my wife left, all I had was the assurances of some friends and a counselor that I would survive. I am a miracle—still in progress. The healing and the growing are still happening. If someone had told me that because of this awful event I would grow, that I would write books, conduct seminars in 40 cities each year, and have a film series, I would have laughed hysterically.

But miracles can happen to those who dare to believe. And sometimes they sneak up on you when you least expect it.

You need to give miracle making some help, some assistance. You need to provide an arena in which it can do its work most effectively. You need to cooperate.

Ask yourself one question: What am I going to do today that will lead me a step closer to my miracle?

General Motors recently announced plans to build a multibillion dollar car plant in Spring Hill, Tennessee, 30 miles from Nashville. Hundreds of cities had fought to be chosen.

GM will bring an economic miracle to the middle of Tennessee. But it will happen only because some people had done their part to "grease the pan" for the development. There had to be available land, highways, schools, and hospitals. It was only when everything was in place that the miracle ignited.

Take a good look at your life. Are there some areas in which you could take charge? What decisions could you make today that might pave the way for the miracle you need?

47   Renewing Your Faith

Faith is a big part of surviving a divorce. Tragically, many find there is no comfortable place for them in the church. Had their mates died, they would have been entitled to Hallmark cards, floral spray, casseroles, a note in the bulletin or newsletter, and a pastoral visit. As a divorced person? Nothing.

Divorced people have to struggle to redefine their place in a congregation. Silence wounds, as does the statement, "I don't know what to say."

How do you overlook the obvious slights?

Divorce can be a laboratory through which your faith is tested and strengthened. You may need to change churches. Some people vow to "change a few attitudes around here." They may only find themselves emotionally and spiritually battered.

Many people reject God during their divorce. Some even blame God for it. Maybe it's time to reexamine your understanding of God. I believe that God weeps with us. God is there, in our pain. It becomes *God's* pain, too.

"Then why doesn't God do something?" you may ask. God is doing something. But it's on God's time line. We want instant relief and instant cures. We're overwhelmed by clocks and second hands. God, however, looks to the future. But God also rescues us from the past and reserves a future for us.

God doesn't make junk. And in the very heart of God, a dream for you persists. "Neither death nor life, neither angels nor demons, neither the present nor the future, nor any powers, neither height nor depth, nor anything else in all creation [not even divorce!] will be able to separate us from the love of God that is in Christ Jesus our Lord" (Rom. 8:38-39).

God will befriend you. We have a God who:

- applauds small but faltering steps.
- who would use this hurt to show you new insights into yourself.
- who is committed to mosaics. You can't make stained-glass windows out of whole sheets of glass. The most beautiful windows come from the smallest broken pieces.

Frederick Buechner said it wonderfully: "In love he made me, in love he will mend me!"

God waits your invitation. God won't come barging into your mess like the cavalry. But if invited, even you will be surprised by God's craftsmanship!

---

48   *Reaffirming Your Value*

I am precious!

Precious is a rare word in our culture. We talk about precious metals or jewels. We sometimes respond (especially grandparents) to a child's words or actions by saying, "Isn't that precious?"

A few fathers have called their daughters "precious" as a temporary but affectionate nickname.

Webster defines *precious* as "of great value or high price; highly esteemed or cherished."

When was the last time you were told "You are precious!" Can you remember? Probably not during the divorce process.

By now you may think that you are the total opposite of precious. Maybe your ex has a few terms he or she likes to share.

Name-calling is tacky business. As children we chanted, "Sticks and stones may break my bones, but words will never hurt me!" Few divorced people say that. We know differently. Words, tones, and inferences can wound and maim. And like imbedded shrapnel, some can infect us long afterward.

But you *are* precious. Yes, you are! Don't argue with me. You are of great value.

Why is that so hard to accept? to believe? List the reasons:

1. _____

2. _____

3. _____

You still haven't changed my mind. The whole Christian faith stands on my side: you are precious.

Why is gold so precious? Because people decided it was. I have a friend named Carl who is divorced and wiser because of it. After his divorce he dated a woman from a very conservative family. She had never been married. At Christmas he went to visit her family, picking a night when aunts and uncles were present. Everyone seemed pleasant and polite. Later, while in the bathroom, he happened to overhear a hallway conversation.

"Isn't it too bad that Kate has to settle for a 'used man'?"

Used doesn't sound all that bad. But Carl insists it was the tone of voice that wounded him.

Or I think of Jane—a woman who still had the tire tracks on her. She thought she was garbage. "Who would want *me*?" she asked herself. So she never dated. She never gave men a chance to reject her.

Then she met Steve, a country boy who loved life. He talked to her and urged her to go out to some singles' group activities— boating, swimming, a few picnics. Nothing threatening.

Slowly she grew to trust him. It took a lot of risk, patience, and time on Steve's part. But he had X-ray eyes. Through the thickness he could see her preciousness.

Slowly, "it took."

They wrote their own ceremony. There were few dry eyes when Steve vowed, "I, Steve, take you, Jane, *as you are.* . . ." Jane is not the same woman today. Steve's love has restored her sense of preciousness.

That's why you can't sleep around. Not because you are a prude, but because you are precious! of high value! Don't finish yourself off. Too many divorced people have chosen life-styles that finished off what their ex initiated.

Maybe you haven't always known that you were precious, or at least acted like you've known it. Maybe you've ignored it. But the fact remains: You *are!*

Now repeat with me: "I, _____ (*insert name*), am precious!" Repeat that 10 times. It's the truth.

49   *Reclaiming Your Dream*

I can "befriend" my past!

"Whatever happened to so-and-so?" Because of the power of the media, a musician or group can have a number one hit, a writer can have a best-seller, or an actor can have a top-rated show, and then completely disappear from view. Baseball players retire; Olympians get older. Politicians lose elections and disappear; celebrities come and go.

The same thing happens with dreams. Margie quit college in her junior year to support her husband while he finished. They agreed that when he finished she would go back. However, she became pregnant. Then she had a second baby. Finally, after years of diapers and runny noses and peanut butter sandwiches, she finished her B.A. Then the marriage unraveled.

In her hurt she considered some possibilities. In lieu of long-term alimony and child support, she opted for two-year support while she went to grad school and earned an M.A. in Marriage and Family Counseling. Today she is a professional counselor, making a big difference in people's lives. She reclaimed her dream.

Who knows how many dreams get mothballed each year?

The U.S. government has found it wise to recall some ships from mothballs and refit them with the latest electronic hardware. We invested too much in them to let them rust.

My guess is that you have some buried dreams. Maybe you buried them to avoid the teasing. "Why, that is the dumbest idea I've ever heard of," or, "You? Go back to school? Ha!" Well, now may be the perfect time to reclaim your dream.

People older than you have gone back to high school, college, or professional school. School was a chance to gain resources to underwrite their dream.

Admittedly, it can take a lot of guts to reclaim a dream. And some people are "dream-busters."

- I don't think I would do that if I were you!
- You've got more guts than I do. . . .
- I don't think it's the right time. . . .

How many people have stayed on a job they hated (regardless of the pay) for fear of failing in starting their own business?

Maybe you can't reclaim your entire dream. But what about a good healthy chunk?

Ken always dreamed of going to med school. But he got married and began teaching. His dream persisted. After his divorce he wanted to take a shot at it, even though:

- he was in debt;
- he would be competing against younger candidates;
- he had become mentally lazy.

Ken developed a strategy. First he eliminated his debt. Then he built a nest-egg. After that he enrolled in two college "refresher" classes taught at night, one in biology and one in chemistry. That also improved his social life, because he found several women to date.

By the time he paid off his bills, he had aced his MSAT scores and three med schools had accepted him.

Dreams. Everyone has dreams, but how many of us are willing to give our dreams a fair footing? Sure, divorce makes it more complicated or drawn out, but who wants a pushover dream? I don't.

What about it? Do you feel the tug of your dream? Sometimes I've lost my kite in the clouds, but it has a way of reminding me that it's still up there.

Remember, for every bubble-burster there will be a cheerleader.

So how about dusting off the old dream? A baby step today might pay incredible dividends tomorrow.

50   *Reserving the Best*

Jimmy Carter, then governor of Georgia, launched his presidential campaign with a question and a book: *Why Not the Best?* What a great question for divorced people to wrestle with as well. You will have choices, decisions, and opportunities, so "Why not the best *for me*?"

You may protest, "I've made such a mess of things!" So what? Abraham Lincoln lost out so many times that today he wouldn't even be considered a good candidate.

- He lost his job and was defeated for the legislature in 1832.
- He failed in business in 1833.
- He lost his sweetheart in 1835.
- He suffered a nervous breakdown in 1836.
- He was defeated for Congress in 1843.
- He was defeated for the Senate in 1854.
- He was defeated for the vice-presidential nomination in 1856.
- He was defeated for the Senate in 1858. [15]

But in 1860 he was elected president of the United States! Many people thought he was a loser. But few other occupants of 1600 Pennsylvania Avenue have left such a legacy. Why? Because his failures sharpened him.

If someone asked me for the book that has most shaped my

life, without hesitation I would answer, *With No Fear of Failure* by Thomas Fatjo and Keith Miller (Word, 1981). That book totally changed my goals and priorities and taught me to look for the *best* rather than just for the good.

Fatjo asks you to list your goals and priorities for three months, one year, and five years and carry the lists in your datebook or checkbook. Then when someone offers you a deal that "you can't say no to," you can in fact say, *no*. Why? Because you have established your priorities.

You need to ask, Does *this* opportunity have *my* initials on it?

That's been the problem with some of the corporate mergers. Corporations have bought companies totally alien to their tradition. Some have then had to "bail out" quickly.

Can you be talked into adapting or mimicking someone else's priorities? Already in this divorce process you've gotten a lot of free advice. People will tell you, "I wouldn't . . .

- quit my job;
- go back to school;
- move;
- buy a new car.

How are you handling all that unsolicited advice? Some of your friends are convinced they are the E. F. Huttons of the emotions. They think that when they give advice, everyone ought to listen.

A friend introduced me to the "best" diet. I've tried all the others; why not this one? It has one simple concept: you can eat anything you want as long as it is *the best*.

I love cookies—especially when I'm thinking about sex or I'm lonely or uptight and need a distraction. Sometimes a whole bag is not enough. There is a grocery store three minutes from my house. When the cookie blues hit I can be wolfing down cookies within five minutes of the first wave.

So I ask myself the question: "Is this cookie the best?" If not, I don't want it. I will wait until I can have the best.

That's "delayed gratification." Oddly enough, it works. It cuts down on cookies. And it will work with other things as well, like desserts or cheap clothes purchased on impulse.

Wait for the best. Do you really need a date that badly? Do you want to marry the first person who knocks at your door? Some dateless weekends are better than the alternatives.

That's why so many sexual "opportunities" need to be passed up. They're not the best. They *can't* be the best! Give your hormones a chance to "age." Why not the best? You deserve it!

51   *Reducing the Emotional Baggage*

I can schedule a memory "garage sale."

Garage sales. Estate sales. Auctions. Junkaramas. Flea markets. Whatever you call them, Americans love 'em. We're accumulators, collectors, savers. Eventually we run out of space. Our attics, closets, basements, and garages are full. We risk an avalanche by simply opening the door!

So we sell, barter, and trade, yelling, "It's a steal at that price!" Occasionally we plead, "What would you give me for it?"

Many divorced people are loaded down with excess emotional baggage: trinkets, hurts, wounds, insults, slights from the marriage, and more from the separation and divorce. Like the dinner party your ex was invited to—and you weren't. Like the fear that you can sense in friends who think you are going to "move in" on their spouses.

Ever wonder why some people don't go when a traffic light turns green? I think they might be digging through their emotional garbage. Some spend a lot of time rearranging, consolidating, trying to get one more item in.

I've been fascinated as I have read accounts of pioneers on the Overland Trail to Oregon. Initially they had to pick and choose what they loaded in the wagon. But often, somewhere along the trail, they had to throw away more items to lighten the wagon on a mountain trail or to ford a stream. The practical always took precedence over the sentimental. The prairies were littered with abandoned furniture and goods because the load became too heavy for the horses to pull.

It's the same way with your collection of emotional baggage.

Ironically, you may not even be aware of what's there. One day you reach for something, and you realize that your ex got it in the settlement. So you either fuss and fume or go buy another one.

It is amazing what people will fight over. The strangest story I have heard is about the moose head contested by a couple in Nashville. He shot it and she had it stuffed as a Christmas present. When he moved out he wanted the moose head to decorate his new place. No way. So they fought. In court she protested that if the moose were removed, the wall would have to be repapered—at his expense. He caved in.

Another couple fought it out over a giant pickle jar full of nuts, bolts, and screws.

Amazing? Or could you name something more bizarre that you or your ex thought was valuable? Initially you may have fought for every inch. Now you wonder why. Some decide to donate any contested items to the Salvation Army Thrift Store.

Others pride themselves on how well they divided their possessions. But what about the emotional baggage? You may need to toss some things in order to lighten your load and ensure survival.

Our Creator only gave us a reasonable amount of storage space—a reasonable amount of tolerance for stress. God doesn't want me bragging about "how broad my shoulders are." God wants us to have light loads for long journeys. That's why God gave us brains.

Do yourself a favor. Check out your shipping manifest. Lighten the load! Besides, letting go of the past makes more room for the great future you have ahead.

52 *Renegotiating Your Future*

The future. "Ah, I don't have time to deal with the future. I'm too busy trying to survive today" moans Sally. But Sally—if you're not concerned about your future, who will be?

Divorced people have to believe in tomorrow. Your future will not be determined by your ex or your past. It's *your* decision. Dr. Frank Freed, a California psychologist, noted, "If it's to be, it begins with *me!*"

There's nothing I can do about yesterday except let it spoil a perfectly good tomorrow.

Tomorrow is my opportunity to put into practice the lessons that I learned today.

A divorce, an inequitable settlement, or continuing battles over alimony, maintenance, or child support cannot rob you of your future. . . *unless you let them.* Sometimes we have to stand in place and dare to believe—despite all the evidence to the contrary—that we will have a future.

I think of Sam Houston, divorced in 1829 while governor of Tennessee, and forced into exile. Aboard a riverboat headed toward Natchez, he contemplated suicide. But later he told how an eagle "swooped near my head, soaring aloft with wildest screams and then was lost in the rays of the setting sun." Houston assigned a positive interpretation to the omen. "I knew then that a great destiny waited for me in the West." [16]

Texas offered him a second chance, a fresh opportunity to etch his name into history: as governor, general, and United States senator. He defeated the Mexican general Santa Anna and brought Texas into the Union.

Historically, broken engagements were almost as offensive as divorces. A young Ohioian had his engagement broken by a woman named Anne Coleman; 10 days later she died. Her beau wrote: "I may sustain the shock. . .but I feel that happiness has fled from me forever."

Possibly you've said the same thing. However, some friends secured a congressional nomination for the young, brokenhearted man and he ended up the only bachelor president of the United States: James Buchanan. [17] Buchanan and Houston refused to let the past dictate their futures.

You may have to renegotiate the timetable for your dream. There may have to be minor or major adjustments. But the future remains.

Our scent of tomorrow may be our only source of joy today. Yet as one friend quips, "One tomorrow at a time, please." Tomorrows often come with compounded interest. Your future may well be far brighter than you could ever imagine or dare to expect.

The difference between what I am and what I become is *what I do!*

Are you looking for a monogrammed future? There's one waiting for you. And your enthusiastic pursuit of tomorrow will encourage someone else.

There is one verse of Scripture that I wish I could tattoo on the inside of every divorced person's eyelids, so that every time they blink they would see it:

" 'For I know the plans I have for you,' declares the Lord, 'plans to prosper you and not to harm you, plans to give you hope and a future' " (Jer. 29:11).

Part Six

RESOURCES FOR RENEWAL

---

53   Baby Steps

Baby steps. No one expects a baby to walk (or to talk coherently). It's a long process complete with bumps, bruises, whines, and setbacks. But it's a process we allow. There are no shortcuts.

There are those times when a toddler falls—and then that long, suspense-filled moment when the child has to decide: Do I laugh or cry?

Baby steps are essential ingredients to growth. Look at Olympic athletes. We see them in their prime, but what about their baby steps? What about those early losses? setbacks? pulled muscles?

As I write this, Pete Rose is closing in on Ty Cobb's hits-at-bat record. But today Rose was at bat four times for *nothing!* So he'll take a shower, get a good meal and night's sleep, then put on his Cincinnati Reds uniform and take some more swings at the record tomorrow.

Don't be intimidated by another's progress. Your ex may already be remarried. So what? He or she may be just one step closer to another divorce. Remember, remarriage is no proof of wisdom.

I was the "baby" of my family (even though I weighed 285 pounds). I preferred the term "birth-order, last." I had to make friends with the term *baby.*

You have to befriend baby steps. I did my bachelor's degree one semester at a time, and basically a day at a time. Some of the course syllabuses seemed overwhelming and intimidating until I discovered that if I read a chapter at a time, wrote one paper at a time, and passed one test at a time, it was conquerable.

I had to ask, What can I do today? The answer? Read 25 pages; go to the library and gather research for my paper. Slowly, day by day, the work got done.

How did I write this book? I didn't sit down and dictate it. For a long time I wrestled with the idea. I spent a lot of time jotting notes. Then it took almost all of a Fourth of July on the floor of my living room organizing index cards into a logical sequence. Slowly, *I Wish Someone Understood My Divorce* emerged.

The process is the same with divorce. A step at a time, please.

54   *Counseling*

It's amazing what you remember from your childhood. I remember a song from our church that had the phrase, "the arm of flesh will fail you, ye dare not trust your own." That's a good explanation of why professional counseling is so important for the divorced. In many ways it is difficult to find a good counselor, particularly in smaller communities. Good counselors respond authentically and compassionately. They listen to more than just a recital of symptoms.

The choice of a counselor is crucial to the success of the counseling. If I break my leg, I don't have to *like* the physician in the emergency room. But if counseling is going to be effective, I need to be able to relate to the counselor.

How do *you* find a good counselor? Ask your minister or family doctor for a referral. Call your Mental Health Association. Depending on the nature of your need, they may refer you to one of several types of counselors, either in private practice or in a community mental health center.

Remember, these are not "shrinks." How many divorced people have screamed, "I don't need a shrink!" That's right. You need a *stretch*. That's what I call the "helpers"—highly skilled professionals who will help you stretch. Whichever professional you counsel with, remember the counselor's task is "not to weaken the conflict but to strengthen you and your self-awareness so that you may grow in the real world as it is," and not particularly as you *wish* it were.[1]

Helpers are not "Mr. Fix-Its" of the emotions. You will need to give them time and give them yourself in order for counseling to work. Here are the different kinds of helpers:

- *Psychiatrist*—a physician with four years of advanced training emphasizing human behavior who treats mental disorders.
- *Psychologist*—a nonphysician with graduate training in human behavior, usually possessing a doctoral degree, such as a Ph.D.
- *Psychiatric social worker*—an individual trained in providing social and human services. Generally will hold at least a master's degree.
- *Counselor*—a person trained in counseling and guidance who works in the mental health field.
- *Psychoanalyst*—a person, usually a psychiatrist or psychologist, who treats patients by talking with them in an attempt

to bring their unconscious conflicts and defenses to the surface.
- *Therapist*—a person trained in a variety of therapeutic techniques for dealing with human behavior.[2]

Ann Laycock Chappel suggests,

It is important to select a helper whose personality is compatible with that of a patient. The helper who is fantastic for one's ex may not be right for one's self. It helps to think of people who have been supportive in one's life. It may be someone 'just like Mom or Dad' or exactly the opposite. Some individuals need an articulate, verbal therapist. Others should have a warm, outgoing personality. A quiet introspective helper may be necessary for maximum trust and open communication in certain instances.[3]

You should be cautious in comparing counselors: "My counselor told me. . . . " Good counselors tailor an approach to help the individual. Helping divorced people is not like dispensing the same prescription for every cold.

It takes courage to make an appointment with a counselor.

It takes courage to go to the first appointment.

It takes courage to return and keep going.

Making an appointment with a counselor could be one of the wisest investments you have ever made.

Yes, it will cost money. But it costs money to have your broken leg set in a cast. So why not spend money for a broken heart? or a mangled hope?

Here are some questions to consider before you make a commitment to a particular counselor-helper:

- Was it easy to talk to this counselor?
- Did the counselor show genuine respect for me?
- Did the counselor ask questions about all the aspects of my life or primarily my divorce?

- Did the counselor project the attitude of knowing "all the answers" or offer 1, 2, 3 solutions?
- Did the counselor imply that he or she is a more "together" person than I am?
- Can I trust the counselor with my secrets?

A counselor is there to help you wrestle with the past, survive the present (even if it is a mess), and help you embrace the future that has your initials on it.

Do yourself a big favor: get some counseling. It's the best thing that happened to me during my divorce.

---

55   A Friend

"He who refreshes others will himself be refreshed" *(Prov. 11:25).*

No one is ever hopelessly depressed in the presence of a friend.

In the Bible, Job had two problems. The first, of course, was his boils. The second was his "comforters." Despite their good intentions, they failed to comfort him.

You've probably experienced the same. The people who come "armed for bear" with scripture verses and 1, 2, 3s and stories about how their Aunt Lucille overcame her depression.

But a friend—a real friend—makes a difference!

I remember my first Thanksgiving as a single. I was deeply

depressed, because Thanksgiving had always been a special occasion. We always joined several couples for a mini-vacation at a lakefront cabin. There was a routine: chili on Wednesday night, a hike on Thursday morning, the big turkey at noon, and Rook and naps all afternoon.

Thanksgiving 1975 was a day to grieve. But I decided to be brave. So I went to the community Thanksgiving service and sang the four verses of *"We Gather Together."* As I looked around the crowded sanctuary, I saw couples—everywhere. Husbands and wives. They looked happy. The longer the service lasted, the deeper I sank into my depression. I drove home needing windshield wipers for my eyes.

But as I walked into my townhouse, turkey smells filled the air. Several families on faculty row were pitching in for a combined meal. My oven had been "volunteered" for the turkey. The neighbor coordinating the event apparently heard my VW pass. She called on the telephone.

"How's the turkey?" she asked. Did she mean me or the one in the oven? I couldn't force an answer through the thick lump in my throat. She repeated the question. Then she asked, "Are you all right?" I groaned. "Do you want Dan to come over?"

"No!" I snapped. I didn't want Dan to see me crying, again.

A few minutes later there was a knock on my back door. Dan walked in. "Linda thought I ought to check on the turkey." Dan peered into the oven with a bewildered look that told me he didn't know what he was supposed to be looking for. Then he sat down on my couch and said, "Maybe I'd better check it again . . . in a few minutes."

So we sat in silence. But slowly, like fog responding to a gentle breeze, my depression cleared. Ten minutes later we carried the turkey down to their house and had a feast with all the trimmings.

Dan is mathematically inclined. He's not exactly a "comforter." But that day he simply cared for me as a friend. He offered no suggestions, no solutions, and quoted no Scriptures. He simply sat there as I cried out my depression.

You don't have to have little letters after your name or certificates hanging on the wall or speak psychobabble or quote preselected Scriptures. Sometimes a friend just sits there, waiting with you.

To this day, I've never had turkey that tasted so wonderful or a friend as faithful as Dan. When he reads this he will shake his head and say, "That was nothing. All I did was sit there waiting for the turkey to be done!"

But that cold Thanksgiving day, Dan redefined the word *friend* for me. And he taught me that as long as I have at least *one* friend, I am not hopelessly depressed.

---

56   *Time*

"Time heals all wounds." If any cliché ever makes the Cliché Hall of Fame, that one will. Like most sayings, it contains some truth but can be very misleading.

Some people are still waiting for "time" to heal their wounds. Meanwhile, they keep reviewing the old photo albums.

It would be more accurate to say, "I enlist time as one of my resources for healing," or, "I will give time a fair chance to be effective."

Only you can decide if time heals effectively.

Some want instant healing. To be over a divorce—now—immediately. In many cases that is impossible. Certainly it is undesirable. You have made too great a personal investment already. And there are many memories to forget.

For example, Jane's birthday is June 4; our anniversary was September 5. For the first few years, those two dates on my datebook produced some discomfort. Some ex's add fuel to the "if only" thoughts on that day. Finally, I decided to say simply, "Yeah, today is her birthday. I hope she has a good one!" and let it go at that.

Now those days seldom register on my emotional calendar. I'm too busy living, creating new memories.

Let's look at the statement, "If we had still been married this would have been our 15th anniversary." So what? The "if" negates the whole memory. When I discovered one of my friends had a birthday on September 5, I took him and some others to a great restaurant that night. I chose to replace my old memory while recognizing its validity as a special day: my friend's birthday—not my ex-anniversary.

I'm taken with Pete Rose's breaking of Ty Cobb's record of most career hits: 4,191. That's a lot of whacks with a bat. Rose was motivated by Bob Broeg, a sports writer, who told him, "Even when you don't feel like it, Pete, you've got to bear down. There are games that mean nothing, games when you might not feel like hitting, but you have to make those at bat just as important to you."

I'd like to paraphrase Broeg for you: "Even when you don't feel like healing or getting over it, you've got to bear down. There are _____ that mean nothing, days when you might not feel like surviving, let alone healing—but you have to take advantage of every opportunity."

For Rose, that meant 13,746 at-bats (in the rain, in 110 degree weather, when he was battling a flu bug, or an obnoxious pitcher). It meant 20 years of batting.

So give yourself the luxury of time.

Give yourself time before you rush into premature dating.

Give yourself time before you commit to any relationship.

Give yourself a lot of time before you say "I do" again.

Time is your friend, not your enemy!

57   *A Support Group*

Americans are classic joiners. Daily, new organizations spring into existence to compete for membership with existing groups. One of the most beneficial organizations now in existence is the support group. Alcoholics Anonymous paved the way for an openness and acceptance that has encouraged the formation of groups for overeaters, homosexuals, wife-beaters, incest victims, etc.

It is essential for your growth that you get involved in a divorce support group. Jim Smoke, who has long been involved with such groups, gives reasons why this is important. First, such groups are emergency rooms for the newly separated or divorced. Thomas Wolfe once defined *home* as a place where they have to take you in. That's what a support group is. A home. Support groups "provide the care needed to heal hurts and provide a reentry to the world of singleness."[4] Many attribute their survival to the nurture of a support group.

Second, these groups are stabilizers because they provide structure, friendships, social activities, and leadership opportunities. Smoke explains that the support group serves as a doorway which is needed "in our lives, not to lounge in, but to pass through."[5]

One of the benefits of the group is that it provides a place to compare notes. You can rest assured that some member is ahead of you and has already faced a particular situation; and that someone is following your footsteps. Bobbie Reed described one session of a divorced support group:

'. . . and there I was hiding in the bathroom just because Dave's new wife was with him when he came to pick up the kids!' Tammy confessed in a small voice, then laughed sheepishly at herself.

The others in the small discussion group joined in her laughter, *reassuring her* that they understood perfectly. A few minutes later the group mood shifted as another member told about a hurt too recent to be funny. A few wiped away silent tears as they shared in the pain. *As each member opened up to the group, a bond of unity was forged, and each individual felt renewed and strengthened by the caring support of the others.*[6]

We're not called to be lone rangers. Even Kimosabe had his faithful sidekick, Tonto.

Another function of the group is to help you learn the ropes of your singlehood. The support group in essence serves a valuable cultural role simply because divorce has not been recognized as a rite of passage. A support group is not a pity party. Nor is it a social function somewhat less competitive than a singles bar. It is a group of cheerleaders who help individuals to function more effectively in life.

In a good group you will not be manipulated or embarrassed or threatened. Look for a group with effective leadership and an effective track record.

There will be times when the support group touches or bumps tender areas of the soul. Here are some things a good support group will not allow:

- a group member speaking for everyone;
- an individual speaking for another individual in the group;
- someone seeking the approval of a group leader or member before or after speaking;
- someone saying, "I don't want to hurt his feelings so I won't say what I'm thinking";
- an individual saying, "I've always been that way!";
- an individual saying, "I'll wait and it will change";
- any one individual rambling and thereby boring the group.[7]

Not everyone easily adjusts to a group; you may want to attend and remain silent. But in time, if you give the group a chance, you will find yourself looking forward to the next meeting.

**The real benefit of a support group comes
at the meeting when you discover, "I am
not alone in my fears. . . ." It is at that
point that a support group can change a
person's life.**

58   *A Vacation*

There is an old joke, "The devil never takes a vacation." The
punch line is, "and that's what makes him the devil."

**Too many people think they can't afford a
vacation. In reality, you can't afford *not* to
take a vacation.**

I'm not talking about a travel agent's definition of *vacation.*
One of those "do-it-all," two-week trips after which you need a
week to recover physically and six months to recover financially.

By *vacation* I mean to vacate the usual, the habitual.

Tragically, a lot of divorced people, particularly single parents,
use up vacation days when they have exhausted their sick leave.
Or they use their vacations to do fix-up projects around the house.

- Vacations are psychological necessities.
- Vacations stretch our minds and rejuvenate our spirits.
- Vacations offer us new, fresh memories.

- Vacations are time outs; they are the bell at the end of a round of boxing.

Tim Hansel devoted two chapters to vacations in his excellent book, *When I Relax I Feel Guilty*. He listed the vacation killers:

- Don't overwait.
- Don't overdo.
- Don't overexpect.

Hansel said, "Since they've waited fifty weeks for this vacation, some people try to cram in a year's worth of living into two weeks . . . rushing from one place to the next, 'hurrying to be happy.' "[8]

Look over his vacation checklist:

1. Have reasonable expectations rather than impossible ones that invariably lead to disappointment.
2. Relax. Let your vacation happen.
3. Expect obstacles (flat tires, etc.).
4. Be creative. Make each vacation a once-in-a-lifetime experience.
5. Take *all* of you on vacation. Use all of your senses.
6. Take short vacations if longer ones are troublesome.
7. Break your routine. Sleep in; read.
8. Plan at least one unusual thing. Be an experimenter. (Besides, these people will never see you again.)
9. Poke some holes in your rigidity.
10. Learn something new on your vacation.
11. Give yourself permission.
12. Live each day and each vacation as if it were your last opportunity.[9]

There may be some memories that try to tag along on your vacation, like the time you and your ex went to X or Y. "We were so happy then!" But remember—that was then and this is now.

You have freedom to design a vacation; you are free to please yourself. Enjoy that freedom. Don't sit at home.

I can hear you protesting. "Vacation? On what? My looks?" Vacations do not have to be extravagant. In fact, you could probably have a good "in-town" vacation. People come from all over the world to Kansas City. Yet although I have lived here seven years, there are dozens of things I have never seen or visited. I bet the same is true of you in your city or town. Hansel argues that vacations do not have to be escapes, but can be introductions. Sometimes what you need is a vacation *to* rather than *from*. He urges, "Travel light, don't spend all your time driving, be a little daring, and enjoy it with all your senses." That sounds un-American.

I personally recommend mini-vacations: one or two day-ers tucked throughout the year. Try one of those motels that advertises, "Spend the night—not a fortune." When I go to Palm Springs I don't stay at some name-brand place where 30% of the cost is going to advertising. I like the Motel 6. It has what I need: a TV, a shower, a bed, towels, air conditioning, an ice machine, and a pool.

Here are two types of vacations you could try:

• *A rest vacation:* go somewhere where no one can find you, take the phone off the hook, and spend most of your days horizontally. Give yourself permission to really relax. Take off your watch. Enjoy.

• *Reinventory vacations.* It's easy to get so busy that we forget what is important: really important. Use this to do some brain exercise:

Start with your lifetime goal. Do you know what it is? Do you know it with enough clarity to write it down? What are some of your lifetime dreams? Your priorities? Are you living in accordance with them these days? How could you improve? It's important to be specific. Take whatever resources along with you that you might need[10] (© 1979; used with permission by David C. Cook Publishing Co.).

I think back to one special California vacation spent at a Motel 6. I took a copy of Denis Waitley's *Seeds of Greatness.* I remember sitting by the side of the pool in the afternoon, reading and thinking. Then I would look away from the book to watch the sun set over the mountains. I enjoyed the gentle swaying of a breeze through those palm trees.

I still remember the crazy vacation when I decided that I could write a novel. Me. That ended up being a vacation with a purpose.

There is something about getting away from the routine that gives us a chance to look with depth at our lives, our jobs, our relationships, and our dreams.

Don't let divorce rob you of a vacation. This may be your chance to begin a whole new chain of memories in the scrapbook of your mind.

59 Exercise

One hundred million Americans are trying to get in shape. Thirty million are joggers (the rest are dodgers of joggers); millions more have paid their bucks to join health clubs, those glorified, air-conditioned, carpeted, torture chambers where singles are stretching, straining, sweating, and meeting!

Health clubs have become the new singles bars of the '80s. You find them all there:

- the lovely narcissists who love the mirrors (and themselves);
- the overweight singles atoning for expense-account lunches and a swinging life-style;
- jilted wives getting in shape for revenge;
- hunky athletes doing battle with iron machines.[11]

Coed health clubs are the new "in" place, not only to sweat but also to evaluate potential partners.

Rolling Stone's Aaron Latham concluded:

The jumps and kicks and sensuous contortions performed are the new dances. The exercise instructors who play records to keep these dances throbbing are the new disc jockeys. Coed health clubs, the new singles' bars of the Eighties, have usurped the sounds and the energy of the discotheques. . . . They have become part of the mating ritual.[12]

Meanwhile, *Jane Fonda's Workout Book* is a runaway best-seller, bought by millions with bulges, droops, and sags, most of whom are looking for a quick, painless way to "the new me."

George Harrar points out that singles can "pick their poison" or obsession:

- 35 million jog regularly;
- 20–30 million swim regularly;
- 35 million ride stationary bikes or use weight machines;
- 6–7 million dance in aerobics;
- 18 million bicycle on weekends.[13]

Someone quipped that he got his exercise as a pallbearer at the funerals of his jogger friends. Yet there is some truth to the need to "survive exercise mania." C. Casey Conrad, head of the President's Council on Physical Fitness, laments:

So many Americans run where they should walk, 'burn' when they should rest, stretch when they should warm up, and pump iron even though they don't know how to lift groceries correctly. . . . The physical fitness revolution has spun off a $3 billion sports-medicine industry.[14]

What should you be doing? An exercise program should have three components:

- *Intensity*—you need to exercise to increase cardiovascular activity—hopefully at the 70% rate.

- *Frequency*—the minimum frequency of exercise should be three times a week; maximum of five.
- *Duration*—each exercise session should last 30-45 minutes.

Do not assume that all that physical activity is permission to eat more. Physical fitness is achieved not through fad diets but through balancing calorie intake with physical exercise.

Here are some diet-helpers:

- *Swimming* develops the heart and lungs and eliminates joint stress. (Besides, all you need is a swimsuit and a towel.)
- *Walking* (with good shoes). Three miles in 45 minutes will be productive. (Next time you have shopping mall-itis— walk instead of buy; it burns calories and helps your bank balance.)
- *Bicycling*.
- *Aerobics*.

Remember, there are also the psychological benefits of exercise. The divorced world is body conscious. If you're sitting at home pigging-out on munchies and trying to soothe your wounds, you're going to gain a lot of weight! That weight will only snafu your healthy self-esteem.

If you are struggling with the divorce "blues," exercise is just what the doctor ordered. During exercise the body releases endorphins into the bloodstream. These are substances that lift our moods.

You don't have to join some expensive health club or buy color-coordinated sweatsuits. Maybe the privacy of your home or apartment is best. Wherever—get started.

60   Reading

Relief may be as close as your library or bookstore. There are hundreds of books on divorce on the market, some of which are capable of making a difference in your life. Buy books or borrow books, but *read* books. It is amazing how many books, purchased with the best of intentions, go unread or half-read.

There hasn't always been such a supply of good reading material. Think about the year 1928, when a young Texas congressman was divorced. It almost ended his political career and wrecked him emotionally. There were no divorce recovery workshops then. Curiosity was rampant. But the congressman followed the advice of Speaker of the House Clark: *read!*

Decades later, this congressman, Sam Rayburn, became the Speaker of the House. He said Clark's advice was "some of the best advice anyone ever gave me." His biographer noted that Rayburn's divorce "faded into his past so deeply that those who knew him years ahead were unaware he had ever been married." Years later, one opponent tried to use it against "Mr. Sam," but "half the people didn't believe it."[15] And Rayburn's protégé, Lyndon Johnson, ended up as president of the United States.

You may not have money to spend on books. Then get a library card. A library is not only a good place to find books, it is a great place to find other resources and to meet people. There are:

● *Record albums and tapes.* Maybe you've only listened to country-western. Try some jazz or some Broadway show tunes.

● *Films or videocassettes* (these can revolutionize your TV habits).

● *Art reproductions.* Some libraries have prints to loan. Tired of looking at "four walls"? Put up a masterpiece.

● *Magazines.* Why have a subscription to a magazine when you can read it free at the public library? Besides, you'll find an incredible number of magazines you've never heard of. They will give you great recipes, ideas, and stories and will stretch your imagination.

● *Seminars.* Libraries are increasingly offering (or providing space for) seminars on child care, money management, travel, taxes, and personal growth.

● *Kiddie corners.* Most libraries have a special section for children. They have story hours or special films for children. Take advantage of it—it's free.

The library is a great alternative to the bar scene. Even if you don't meet the perfect mate in the stacks, you've improved your mind. If you do meet someone, they will most likely be literate.

Finally, get to know your librarians. Just say, "I'm going through a divorce and was wondering if you could recommend some good things for me to read." Not only will they help you with the "how to get over a divorce" type books, they will be familiar with some novels that touch on themes related to divorce and single parenting.

Scripture talks about "renewing your mind." Your library card is a passport to a new you. Take advantage of that.

Read.

AFTERWORD: YOUR DIVORCE CAN MAKE A DIFFERENCE

We have come to the end of our journey. Now you must begin writing the next chapter. How will you finish this statement:

My divorce _____

_____

It's still early. Regardless of yesterday, each of us has a today. Whose permission are you waiting for? Catch your breath. Reshape your dream. Then go for it.

Basil Pennington, a Trappist monk, told a story about a Syrian rabbi named Zuscha. On his deathbed someone asked Zuscha what he thought the kingdom of God was going to be like. The old rabbi thought for a long time before answering.

"I don't know," he finally said. "But one thing I do know: When I get there, I am not going to be asked, 'Why weren't you Moses?' or 'Why weren't you David?' I am going to be asked, 'Why weren't you Zuscha?' "[16]

It's always too early to quit!

It's never too late to begin!

Give growth a chance. Be you!

You have walked through hell and emerged "tested"—perhaps wiser, more confident, more aware of how great it is to be alive.

Now the second stage begins. You must help other people heal. Because you have survived, you have an obligation to help those whose "today" resembles a day in your past. They are as confused, frustrated, angry, and broken as you were.

If real healing happens, they will need someone who has emerged from the wilderness and can walk with them along the way.

Someone needs you to be with them. Someone needs you to make a difference. Someone needs you to understand.

NOTES

Part One: It's Happening!

1. Eugene Kennedy, *Sexual Counseling: A Practical Guide for Non-Professional Counselors* (New York: Continuum, 1977), p. ix.
2. Jim Smoke, *Living Beyond Divorce* (Eugene, Ore.: Harvest House, 1984), p. 14.
3. Denis Waitley and Reni L. Witt, *The Joy of Working* (New York: Dodd, Mead, 1985), p. 267.
4. Ibid., p. 243.
5. Ibid., p. 145.

Part Two: "I Wish Someone Understood"

1. Jim Lutz, presentation on single parenting, First Baptist Church, Parkersburg, Va., April 3, 1982.
2. Nicki Scott, *Louisville Courier-Journal*, December 14, 1982.
3. Steven Hicks, "Off the Wall," *One* 1 (May-June 1984): 16.
4. Lenore J. Weitzman, *The Divorce Revolution: The Unexpected Social and Economic Consequences for Women and Children in America* (New York: Free, 1985), p. 323.
5. Waitley and Witt, p. 46.
6. Ibid.
7. Max Rheinstein, *Marriage Stability, Divorce and the Law* (Chicago: University of Chicago Press, 1972), p. 28.
8. Henry James, Horace Greeley, and Stephen Pearl Andrews, *Love, Marriage, and Divorce and the Sovereignty of the Individual: A Discussion* (Boston: Benjamin R. Tucker, 1889), p. 24.
9. James G. Powers, *Marriage and Divorce* (New York: American News Company, 1870), p. 105.
10. Frank R. Tillapaugh, *The Church Unleashed* (Ventura: Regal, 1982), p. 147.
11. David R. Mace and Vera Mace, *What's Happening to Clergy Marriages* (Nashville: Abingdon, 1980), p. 24.

Part Three: Barriers to Understanding

1. Ann Romberger, "Janet Nelson: The Pragmatic Path," *Harvard Divinity School Bulletin* 15 (March 1985): 13.
2. Paul Hauck, *Overcoming Depression* (Philadelphia: Westminster, 1973), p. 24.

Part Four: Dealing with Fears

1. Wayne E. Oates, *Pastoral Care and Counseling in Grief and Separation* (Philadelphia: Fortress, 1976), pp. 48–49.
2. Bob Benson, *Musings* (April 1, 1985), p. 2.
3. Oates, *Pastoral Care and Counseling*, p. 48.

4. Doug C. Kimmel, *Adulthood and Aging* (New York: John Wiley, 1974), p. 221.
5. Carolyn Koons, lecture, "Change," July 28, 1985.
6. "The Single Parent's Family Album," *Newsweek* (July 15, 1985), p. 48.
7. Alice Stolper Peppler, *Single Again: This Time with Children* (Minneapolis: Augsburg, 1982), pp. 103–108.
8. Advertisement, *Time*, September 1, 1980.
9. Joseph Procaccini and Mark Kiefaber, *Parent Burnout* (New York: Doubleday, 1983). Quoted in "High Achievers Are Candidates for Burnout," *Miami Herald*, August 1, 1985.
10. Marilyn Elias, *USA Today*, September 9, 1985.
11. Ray E. Short, *Sex, Dating, and Love* (Minneapolis: Augsburg, 1984), p. 99.
12. Ibid., p. 101.
13. Bud and Kathy Pearson, *Single Again: Remarrying for the Right Reasons* (Glendale: Regal, 1985), p. 70.
14. Andrew Greeley, *The Cardinal Sins* (New York: Warner, 1981), p. 84.
15. Weitzman, *The Divorce Revolution*, p. 325.
16. Ibid.
17. Larry Burkett, "Your Money in Changing Times," *Your Finances*, November 1984, p. 2.
18. Nicki Scott, *Louisville Times*, September 15, 1983.
19. Ibid.
20. Barbara S. Cain, "The Gray Divorcees," *The Louisville Courier-Journal Magazine*, February 20, 1983, pp. 24–26.
21. Ibid.
22. Ibid.
23. Cited by Louise Bernikow, "Life in the Alone Zone," *Mademoiselle*, August 1985, p. 224.
24. Ibid.

Part Five: Priorities for Living

1. Richard Gerber, "Selected Theological Implications in Divorce: Learning from an Unwelcomed Experience," *Theological Markings* 13 (Summer 1984): 14-18.
2. Ibid.
3. Arthur W. Calhoun, *A Social History of the American Family*, vol. 1, *The Colonial Period* (New York: Barnes and Noble, 1917), p. 138.
4. Charlie W. Shedd, *If I Can Write, You Can Write* (Cincinnati: Writer's Digest Books, 1983), p. 137.
5. Alan Jones, *Exploring Spiritual Direction* (New York: Seabury, 1982), p. 42.
6. Ray Short, *Sex, Love, or Infatuation* (Minneapolis: Augsburg, 1978), p. 29.
7. Short, *Sex, Dating, and Love*, p. 45.
8. Gerald G. Jampolsky, *Love Is Letting Go of Fear* (Millbrae, Calif.: Celestial Arts, 1979), p. 19.
9. Cited in Helen Gurley Brown, *Having It All* (New York: Simon and Schuster, 1982), p. 374.
10. Waitley and Witt, *The Joy of Working*, p. 208.
11. Ibid.
12. C. S. Lewis, *A Grief Observed* (New York: Seabury, 1961), p. 63.

13. Jason Towner, *Jason Loves Jane but They Got a Divorce* (Nashville: Impact, 1978), p. 164.
14. Waitley and Witt, *The Joy of Working*, p. 195.
15. Waitley and Witt, *The Joy of Working*, pp. 57–58.
16. Marquis James, *The Raven: The Story of Sam Houston* (Indianapolis: Bobbs-Merrill, 1929), p. 85.
17. George Ticknor Curtis, *Life of James Buchanan*, vol. 1 (New York: Harper and Row, 1883), pp. 19, 18.

Part Six: Resources for Renewal

1. Oates, *Pastoral Care and Counseling*, p. 13.
2. Winifred Scheffler, "Mental Health Care: Editorial Research Reports," in *Congressional Quarterly* 2 (September 21, 1979): 691.
3. Ann Laycock Chappel in Ann Landers, *The Ann Landers Encyclopedia, A–Z* (New York: Doubleday, 1978), p. 892.
4. Smoke, *Living Beyond Divorce*, p. 120.
5. Ibid.
6. Bobbie Reed, *Single on Sunday* (St. Louis: Concordia, 1979), p. 44.
7. Wayna W. Dyer and John Vriend, *Group Counseling* (New York: Simon and Schuster, 1980), pp. 118–119.
8. Tim Hansel, *When I Relax I Feel Guilty* (Chicago: David C. Cook, 1979), p. 110. Copyright © 1979, David C. Cook Publishing Co. Used with permission.
9. Ibid., pp. 112–114.
10. Ibid., p. 118.
11. Gay Talese, "Men and Women Are Working Out, but Are They Working It Out?" *Esquire*, November 1984, p. 90.
12. Aaron Latham, "Perfect! Coed Health Clubs Are the Singles' Bars of the Eighties," *Rolling Stone*, June 9, 1983, p. 20.
13. George Harrar, "Getting the Right Fit," *American Way*, November 1983, p. 186.
14. Alfred Steinberg, *Sam Rayburn: A Biography* (New York: Hawthorn, 1975), p. 51.
15. Ibid.
16. M. Basil Pennington, *Centered Living: The Way of Centering Prayer* (New York: Doubleday, 1986), p. 102.